The Vindication of Tradition

The 1983 Jefferson Lecture in the Humanities

The Vindication of Tradition,

J.

JAROSLAV PELIKAN

Yale University Press
New Haven and London

Designed by Nancy Ovedovitz and set in VIP Palatino type by The Saybrook Press, Inc. Printed in the United States of America by Vail-Ballou Press, Binghamton, New York.

Library of Congress Cataloging in Publication Data
Pelikan, Jaroslav Jan, 1923–
    The vindication of tradition.
    (The 1983 Jefferson lecture in the humanities)
    Includes bibliographical references.
    1. Learning and scholarship—Addresses, essays, lectures. 2. Tradition (Philosophy)—Addresses, essays, lectures. I. Title. II. Series: Jefferson lecture in the humanities; 1983.
    AZ103.P44   1984   001.2   84-5132
    ISBN 0–300–03154–8 (alk. paper)

The paper in this book meets the guidelines for permanence and durability of the Committee on Production Guidelines for Book Longevity of the Council on Library Resources.

1   3   5   7   9   10   8   6   4   2

To the memory of my parents—
and to my children.

Was du ererbt von deinen Vätern hast,
Erwirb es, um es zu besitzen.

What you have as heritage,
Take now as task;
For thus you will make it your own!

Goethe, *Faust*

Contents

Preface

The invitation of the National Endowment for the Humanities to deliver the Jefferson Lecture for 1983 gave me what was in many ways an ideal opportunity for some systematic reflecting on my lifelong study of continuity and change in the development of tradition. What I am presenting in these lectures, therefore, is not primarily historical research into that development. That I have done *in extenso* elsewhere, particularly in *The Christian Tradition: A History of the Development of Doctrine*, four of whose five volumes have now appeared. In the notes to the lectures I have for that reason cited those volumes, as well as other works of my own, much more frequently than is my wont. I have also concentrated the documentation and the bibliographical references for the entire series of four lectures in the notes to the first two lectures, in order to lay the foundation for the affirmations of the final two.

Following the example set by several of my predecessors in the Jefferson Lectureship, I have, in this written form, striven to retain the flavor of lectures (except, of course, for purely topical references), complete with an unusually extensive use of what a friend of mine calls "the first person perpendicular."

For rhetoric, too, has an honorable place in the traditions I am describing and celebrating here, and it is fitting that the readers of the book should hear occasional echoes of the lecture hall.

The lecture halls in which this material was presented between May and September of 1983 were, in chronological order, the auditorium of the National Academy of Sciences in Washington, D.C., the Glen Lloyd Auditorium of the University of Chicago, the Herbst Theater War Memorial in San Francisco, the Seeley G. Mudd Building of the University of Southern California in Los Angeles, and the Sheldonian Theatre of the University of Oxford. To all my hosts and hearers at those places, and above all to Chairman William Bennett of the National Endowment and his colleagues, I am profoundly grateful.

ONE

The Rediscovery of Tradition

A Progress Report

erhaps as appropriate a way as any to identify the theme of these Jefferson Lectures would be to begin with an anecdote from Richard Altman's story of how *Fiddler on the Roof* evolved from the stories of Sholom Aleichem into the Broadway musical and worldwide success it eventually became:

> I don't know who finally made the discovery that the show was really about the disintegration of a whole way of life, but I do remember that it was a surprise to all of us. And once we found that out—which was pretty exciting—[Jerome] Robbins said, *"Well, if it's a show about tradition and its dissolution, then the audience should be told what that tradition is."* . . . "Tradition" was the key to *Fiddler's* meaning.

As it turned out, the opening song and dance number, "Tradition," was also for many the most memorable part of the show—except perhaps for Tevye's expostulations with the

Almighty, in "If I Were a Rich Man," about the mysteries of His celestial plan.

Jerome Robbins was absolutely right in his intuition: "If it's a show about tradition and its dissolution, then the audience should be told what that tradition is." Analogously, if the intellectual history of the West since the Renaissance or since the Enlightenment is also "about tradition and its dissolution," then the audience for which scholars write or tell that history, in whole or in part, likewise "should be told what that tradition is." Until quite recently, it may have been possible to assume some knowledge of that tradition in our audience. Thus if one accepts at face value what the articles in the monumental eleventh edition of the *Encyclopædia Britannica* seem to be taking for granted in their audience, readers who belonged to that social and educational class were expected to be able to decipher Greek and Latin, but, more important, to recognize allusions to the Greek and Roman classics and to the Bible without having to be told each time which books belonged to each of these canons and why it was that they were expected to know these books in the first place.

There was undoubtedly some self-deception and some fakery (as well as some snobbery) in this assumption. Speaking as an editor and contributor for the fourteenth edition, I know very well how easy it is to romanticize the eleventh edition of the *Britannica* (which was able to allot four times as much space to John Malcolm Mitchell's article "Delian League" as to the unsigned article "Uranium"), as well as its supposed readership. But one has only to read, for example, the papers of Frederick Douglass, now being edited by Professor John Blassingame and being published by the Yale University Press, to see the ease with which that intellectual and moral leader of the Black community alluded to the Bible, to the Old Testament more perhaps even than to the New, as he related the experience of his audience to this essential component of their collective tradition—all the more effectively because it was also affirmed in theory, though often denied in practice, by their oppressors.

Whatever validity such an expectation about the audience may have had in those preceding generations, anyone who teaches undergraduates, as I do, or for that matter anyone who teaches theological students, as I used to, will attest that it is pedagogically foolhardy to make any such assumptions today. I could list various howlers from student papers, but I am indebted to Studs Terkel for the best anecdote of all. Recently, when he chided a group of students for having no sense of tradition and for supposing that the history of music begins with Bob Dylan, one of them asked him: "Bob who?" But after the amusement subsides, we are left with a crucial intellectual and educational problem: in the words of Jerome Robbins, "then the audience should be told what that tradition is." Otherwise the history of the loss of the tradition will not make sense, nor will any other chapter of our common history.

Fortunately, we are not bereft of intellectual and scholarly resources for addressing the issue. These past several decades may have been a period during which the home, the community, the school, and the church have all declined gravely in their ability (or willingness) to transmit one or another constituent element of the tradition. But those very same years have also been a period in which humanistic scholarship in various fields has been rediscovering "tradition." The rediscovery involves the concept of tradition itself as a category and method of research, as well as the content of various specific traditions.

Thus we are, on this level at any rate, better equipped to deal with tradition than were our scholarly predecessors, although they and their audiences may have had a better concrete grasp of one or another of the specific traditions than we do.

Much of the credit for this achievement belongs to the coming of age, during this same period, of the social sciences, above all of anthropology. Its empirical studies of various societies, and chiefly of primitive societies, have illumined the role of tradition as the social glue that brings cohesiveness to a clan or tribe. Over and over, researchers in such societies have been told, "That is the way we have always done it," even when the specific custom may in some cases be shown to have been very recent in origin, at least in this precise form. It is, moreover, in custom—a particular way of preparing food, or of initiating the young through the rites of passage into the privileges and responsibilities of adulthood, or of marking the end of life—that some of the tradition most effectively manifests and transmits itself. Such custom is frequently accompanied by traditional formulas of recitation and incantation, which are, in both primitive and developed cultures, often linguistically archaic (as is, for example, the use of *thou* in English) or even (as in the case of Old Church Slavonic) enshrined in a special cultic language no longer commonly used or generally understood. As Eisenstadt and others have pointed out, however, the conventional classification of societies as either *traditional* or *post-traditional* may, despite the undeniably valid point in such a distinction, lead a superficial reader to suppose that therefore such "modern" societies do not have a constructive relation to their own traditions.

Not because the discoveries and insights of anthropology are not relevant to my topic here—for they are—but because I cannot claim anything more than a derivative knowledge of research in the field, I must concentrate on those areas of research in which I myself have worked, which is to say, the traditions and texts that have come down to us in Greek and Latin, and among these primarily the documents of the Christian tradition. Let me begin, however, with some documents that are older, from those periods of Greek literature that antedate the coming of Christianity in Hellenic and Hellenistic form. (Perhaps I may be permitted the reminder that the history of Christian Greek literature is far longer, although also far less distinguished, than is the history of pagan Greek—or, as the savants like to say, "profane Greek"—literature.) One of the most dramatic chapters in the history of the scholarly rediscovery of tradition during the twentieth century was written by the brilliant, but tragically brief, career of Milman Parry.

Ever since F. A. Wolf's *Prolegomena* of 1795, scholars had been attempting to get behind the *Iliad* and the *Odyssey* to their sources, much as, at about the same time, their colleagues were seeking to identify the several sources that have been put together into the Pentateuch and into the Gospels. Sensing the anachronism in the supposition that Homer, whoever he or they may have been, had proceeded in a manner that resembled the work of a modern redactor, Parry chased the Homeric myths into the wilds of what had recently become Yugoslavia, where he found tribesmen still singing and reciting similar epics as they had received them and as they were in the process of handing them on. When the late Rebecca West was in Yugoslavia a couple of years later, in 1937, she experienced the same connection of the Yugoslavs with the Homeric tradition. Her husband reminded her of actions they had witnessed that, he said, "must have been made a million million million

times since the world began," yet seemed "absolutely fresh."
"Well, it is so in the *Iliad*," he continued. "When one reads
of a man drawing a bow or raising a shield, it is as if the dew of
the world's morning lay undisturbed on what he did." Such
a tradition was, if I may adapt the phrase of Augustine, a
"beauty ever ancient, ever new."

The methods of tradition-history, as such study of literature
has come to be called, were applied also to Greek drama and
even to Greek philosophy, by such scholars as Francis Cornford, Jane Harrison, and Gilbert Murray, with results that still
remain highly controversial but also extremely provocative
and productive. When it was applied to the New Testament,
the quest for a tradition within and behind the received text
was responsible for an entire new era in the long history of
biblical interpretation. Since the days of the ancient church,
everyone could see that the writers of the first three Gospels
had used much of the same material but had reworked it in
various ways. But here, too, it is an anachronism to speak of
their reworking the stories and sayings, as though they had
been functioning in an individual capacity rather than in and
for a community. The community had been there first—and so
had the materials. Whichever of the Gospel writers might be
entitled to chronological priority (and it was usually assumed
to be the one who composed the Gospel of Mark), the real
priority belonged to the tradition as such.

It was to this tradition, and not simply to one another, or to
some written source now no longer in existence, that all three
of the synoptic Gospels were to be traced. (From the beginning, everyone had known that the Gospel of John belonged to
a class by itself.) So it came about that during the twentieth
century the scholarly study of the New Testament turned to

"the history of the Synoptic tradition," to use the title of one of
the most influential books on the subject, by Rudolf Bultmann.
That title is all the more interesting in the light of a later essay,
"The New Testament and Mythology," for which Bultmann
has acquired the greatest notoriety and which is in many ways
an attack on the mainstream of the Christian tradition of how
to read the New Testament. Apparently the pre-Gospel tradition (which no longer exists) is a necessary factor in the interpretation of the Gospels, but the post-Gospel tradition in the
church (which exists in thousands of volumes) does not have a
similar standing. But tradition there certainly was, even before
and within the Bible and not simply after the Bible: tradition
was, in Grelot's phrase, the "source and environment of Scripture."

Drawing a sharp distinction between *gospel* and *tradition* had
been a major plank in the platform of the Protestant Reformers. Luther, for example, had the impression, mistaken though
it was, that Tertullian, at the end of the second and the beginning of the third century, was the earliest of the ancient Christian writers after the apostles, so that it was possible to make
the distinction between Scripture and tradition also, though
not only, on chronological grounds. The later historiography
of the Reformation applied the distinction to the teaching of
the Reformers themselves, stressing their "recovery" of the
authentic gospel message and their divergence from the tradition that had developed between the gospel message and the
sixteenth century. There had, to be sure, been "forerunners of
the Reformation," such as Wycliffe and Hus, and some of the
church fathers were regarded as legitimate ancestors of the
Reformation.

More often than not, however, even these forerunners and

ancestors appeared in Protestant histories as a foil for the
Reformers. Contemporary research has, in a number of important ways, revised this standard picture of the relation of the
Reformation to tradition. The most important has been the
gradual illumination of the intellectual history of the fourteenth and fifteenth centuries, which had been the victim of
neglect. Medievalists had tended to be preoccupied with the
age of Francis and Bonaventure, of Thomas Aquinas and
Dante, while Reformation scholars tended to begin their researches within the sixteenth century itself. Many of the most
important thinkers of the two-and-one-half centuries between
Aquinas and Luther (for example, William of Ockham and
Nicholas of Cusa) were not available in any critical edition,
while new editions and translations both of Aquinas and of
Luther went on being published.

Thanks to the dedicated work of the last generation or two of
scholars—European and American, Roman Catholic and Protestant, historians of the church and historians of politics and of
society—we have begun to put the Reformation back into its
historical context, and we are identifying the lines of positive
influence, as well as the lines of divergence, between it and its
tradition. Inspired by those discoveries, other scholars, among
whom I am pleased to be numbered, are also reexamining the
relation between the Reformers and the earlier tradition, look-
ing for those elements in the tradition—for example, the orthodox doctrine of the Trinity—that the thought of Luther and
Calvin presupposed because they were self-evident to them,
though they may not be self-evident today. The resulting
picture of the sixteenth century may be far less tidy, but it may
also be more accurate in its rediscovery of the positive as well
as the negative connections between tradition and Reformation.

An interest in those connections naturally leads to the further question of how the Reformation itself became a tradition in turn. The history of the interpretation of the Reformation over the past four centuries or so is a key to the intellectual history of those lands in which the Reformation was a crucial turning point not only for religion, but for language, literature, education, and politics—lands such as Bohemia, Germany, England and Scotland, and the Scandinavian countries. How, in the nineteenth century, Joseph Priestley or Søren Kierkegaard interpreted Luther belongs to our interpretation of Priestley or of Kierkegaard. For our purposes here, one of the most intriguing aspects of this kind of study is the uncovering of the processes by which the very antitraditionalism of the Reformation has itself become a tradition. After four centuries of saying, in the well-known formula of the English divine, William Chillingworth, that "the Bible only is the religion of Protestants," Protestants have, in this principle, nothing less than a full-blown tradition.

And so the Bible was not "the Bible only" after all. The explosion of historical interest in Puritan theology, set off in large measure by the pioneering researches of Perry Miller, leads to the recognition that there was, and to a great extent still is, a Puritan tradition of biblical hermeneutics. For the Puritan, "the Bible was clear and definite on the form of the church, on the code of punishments for crimes, on the general purposes of social existence; its specifications were binding on all, magistrates, ministers, citizens." Therefore there was a direct application of the Old Testament to contemporary social issues. Only occasionally has a Roger Williams come along to challenge this assumption with the declaration that "no modern community any longer possesses in the physical realm those sanctions with which Israel alone had been invested" and that "therefore the modern magistrate must get along as best he can": the preacher was not authorized to tell the magistrate what to do. But the principle itself, and the method of interpretation, would appear to be "the way we have always done it," that is to say, a tradition.

Thus the scholarly rediscovery of tradition, by supplying at least some of the missing quotation marks, has made us sensitive to the ways in which our past has used its past. Not least has it done so for our understanding of those movements in intellectual history that have repudiated explicit elements of their past but have nevertheless gone on presupposing some of its implicit values. In a lectureship bearing the name of Thomas Jefferson it seems appropriate to point out that what were for him self-evident truths about creation, equality, and inalienable rights were so self-evident at least partly as a consequence of the traditional doctrine of the creation of the human race in the image of God, a doctrine whose roots lie in both Athens and Jerusalem.

Such truths, moreover, have often come to appear far less self-evident when they were plucked from those roots and exported to a culture that did not presuppose these implicit values. In the interest of simple historical justice, however, it is necessary to add the observation that, also in its doctrine of creation in the image of God, the Christian tradition itself has likewise manifested considerable skill at this practice of affirming in the concrete what it denied in the abstract. It denounced Platonism even as it confessed doctrines that it could not have formulated as it did without the illumination of Platonism, thus speaking the language of Zion but with the unmistakable accents of the Academy. Later generations of Christians, who stood in the doctrinal tradition of Jerusalem but could no longer recognize the philosophical accents of Athens, have been obliged to rediscover that other half of their intellectual ancestry.

In much the same way, the genetic inheritance of some ideas and systems which, in our own age, have been seen to be aligned against the Judeo-Christian tradition contains perspectives that were historically derived from, though they need not be philosophically dependent upon, that tradition. Thus William Temple, Nicolas Berdyaev, and other thinkers have maintained that in Marxism the very notion of a historical teleology, according to which the historical process moves by dialectical stages to its intended goal, comes, probably via Hegel, from the Hebrew Bible, with its vision of the divine providence within and yet beyond history. Berdyaev went on to describe how, in the Russian Revolution of 1917, this historical teleology of Marxist teaching was combined with another hybrid descendant of the Judeo-Christian tradition, what he calls the "messianic" interpretation of history and of Russian destiny so characteristic of many Slavophil philosophers and theologians in the second half of the nineteenth century. If this reading of the history is sound, therefore—and I do have some questions about it—it is necessary, in attempting to understand Marxism-Leninism, to see it as, among other things, a kind of Christian heresy. Studies of the problem of "tradition and revolution" by Marxist scholars suggest, however, that they may be beginning to recognize just how profoundly complex this problem is.

In other fields than intellectual history, the implications of the rediscovery of tradition are, if anything, more far-reaching. For example, I have been involved, despite my own total lack of formal scholarly preparation, in the critical review of programs of study, of dissertations, and of scholarly manuscripts in the field of art history, simply because the subject matter for so much of the history of painting, sculpture, and architecture in our tradition has been suggested by the ideas and materials to which I have devoted my research. Thus the typology of Old Testament and New—of the manna in the desert and the Christian Eucharist, or of Joshua and Jesus (the names can be identical in Greek), or of Eve and Mary—sets the pattern for countless mosaics, frescoes, and diptychs, with the Old Testament "promise" on one wall and the New Testament "fulfillment" on the other. Since these pictures are often unlabeled, the key to their identification and interpretation must frequently be sought in the works of the church fathers on biblical exegesis, where the motifs of promise and fulfillment provide one of the most widely used methods for extracting meaning from the Hebrew Bible (albeit in its Greek or Latin version). The *Lives* of the postbiblical saints constitute a remarkable, and now little-known, genre of literature, which is yet another example of the pluralistic origins of the Christian tradition, classical as well as biblical. These *Lives* inspired icons, altarpieces, and other paintings, and were in turn inspired by them. An upsurge of interest in some particular saints, for example in Jerome around the time of Caravaggio, manifests an interaction between art and devotion that is unintelligible without the study of the tradition upon which both art and devotion drew.

How art, devotion, and thought drew upon their traditions is a process deserving of careful study for its own sake. Thanks to Jacob Burckhardt, we have long been accustomed to consider this process in the Italian Renaissance. "The revival of antiquity" was, to at least some of the literary and intellectual leaders of the Renaissance, the most important change going on around them: what was new was a new sense of the old, even a new definition of the old, which brought liberation from the domination of the more recent. But we who teach the intellectual and cultural history of the Middle Ages are now obliged to take account of the several additional "renaissances" that have been discovered—or invented—by scholars: the Carolingian renaissance of the ninth century, to which we owe so many of the manuscripts of antiquity, pagan no less than Christian, on which our knowledge of Western literature depends; the renaissance of the twelfth century attributed by Charles Homer Haskins to the school of Chartres; and the Aristotelian renaissance during the thirteenth century, with its impact on philosophy and on science, and of course on theology. Although this proliferation of renaissances may well rob the term of any specific meaning, the phenomenon does demonstrate that there is a history of history, a tradition of handling and of rediscovering tradition that forms an important chapter in the record of the thousand years between the fall of Rome, "Old Rome," and the fall of Constantinople, "New Rome."

Whatever such rediscoverers of tradition may have supposed they were doing, it is up to us to be sensitive to the reconstruction and revision of the past that any such rediscovery entails, our own rediscoveries no less than theirs. History, Count Paul Yorck wrote to Wilhelm Dilthey, must be "regressive": it is always written backwards, as, in a sense, the present moves forward into its past. Therefore what the sieve of historical study retains, and what it lets fall through, is one of the topics to which our study of the history of history must attend. It is at the same time often a key, or even *the* key, to a system of thought to ask about the selectivity of its interpretation of tradition. Why, for example, did so much (though by no means all) of medieval Aristotelianism in science adopt the conclusions of the master's scientific investigations, rather than his methods, by which those conclusions could have been corrected, and eventually were? By constructing his telescope and using it to observe empirically, Galileo was a more faithful Aristotelian than were those who quoted Aristotle's *Physics* against his observations. Every time a scholar describes the history of the rediscoveries and reinterpretations of some important tradition, as has been done in the histories of the interpretation of the Reformation to which I referred earlier, we can see more both in the tradition itself and in the thought of those whose pictures of the tradition emerge from such a history.

Speaking now for my own research into the history of tradition—but, I would insist, not only for my own research—I would now emphasize, far more than I did when I began my studies, the nonverbal, or at any rate the nonconceptual, element of tradition, together with the words and concepts, ideas and doctrines, that continue to be the final object of my investigation. That change in the job description for the historian of tradition has been forced upon me by the nature of the source material and, to be sure, by the kinds of questions that I, more and more, found myself putting to the source material. According to the greatest of my predecessors in this field, Adolf von Harnack, "another instance of the exceptional nature of Christianity" was that "for quite a time it possessed no ritual at all" and that therefore "the history of dogma during the first three centuries is not reflected in the liturgy."

Therefore Harnack, who in fact knew a great deal about the

early liturgies (as he did about almost everything else in the first three or four centuries of Christian history), proceeded to write the history of what the church had taught without referring very often to how the church had prayed, sung, and celebrated. Repeatedly, by contrast, I have found what a fifth-century theologian, Prosper of Aquitaine, called "the rule of prayer" to be indispensable for the understanding of the history of what he called "the rule of faith." Prosper made this distinction in his defense of Augustine. When Augustine had been challenged by his opponents to substantiate from tradition his novel teaching about human nature, the fall, and original sin, he had appealed from the tradition of theology and philosophy to the tradition of prayer and devotion, where he located the ancestry of a concept that he was now formulating in the modality of theology and philosophy.

For if tradition is "an extension of the franchise" by "giving votes to the most obscure of all classes, our ancestors," then the history of tradition requires that we listen to the choruses and not only to the soloists—nor only to the virtuosi among the soloists. The historical rediscovery of tradition made Milman Parry go beyond the one poet Homer, or the several poets Homer, to the anonymous bards and carriers of the tradition whose legitimate heirs he found among Serb and Croat tribesmen. Of course the virtuoso belongs to the story, and a historian would have to be more ascetic than I am to deny himself the pleasure of listening to a soloist like Augustine.

But listening to Augustine and giving him his historical due means taking him seriously in his incessant declarations of allegiance to the Catholic tradition, the very declarations that so many have found the most troubling in him and have sought to dismiss as not the "real" Augustine. Troubling

though they may be to the theologian, they should be, to the
historian, a guide to how Augustine wished himself to be read,
even at his most subjective: not in isolation from the community of his past and in his present, the community of which
he had finally become a part after all his wanderings, but as a
spokesman for that community.

When now the historian of tradition goes on from Augustine
to Augustinianism, the need to avoid the "great man theory"
of history becomes all the more imperative. Augustine is probably the most influential figure in medieval intellectual history:
as the saying goes, perhaps not the greatest of Latin writers,
but almost certainly the greatest man who ever wrote Latin.
But he is this not only, and not even chiefly, because other
giants of the Middle Ages who might deserve to stand alongside him—Anselm of Canterbury, or Bernard of Clairvaux, or
Thomas Aquinas, or Bonaventure, or John Duns Scotus (to list
them in strictly chronological order)—were all, in one way or
another, Augustinians, as were, for that matter, Luther, Calvin, Pascal, and even, in some sense, Descartes. What is so
impressive about Augustine for our purposes here is that, as
he drew from tradition and not only from Plato and Paul and
other giants, so he also became part of the tradition, for literally millions of men and women who learned to look at the
world and at human life as he had taught them—when not
directly through his writings, which have circulated in millions of copies over the past fifteen centuries, then through the
later catechisms, devotional books, and sermons that drew so
much of their contents from him.

The rediscovery of Augustine was a component of each of
the medieval "renaissances" I enumerated, including the Italian Renaissance itself, when Petrarch confronted Augustine

and thus himself in *My Secret* and atop Mount Ventoux. The Protestant Reformers likewise saw themselves as rediscovering the authentic Augustine after he had been hidden under an Aristotelian cloud in the systems of the scholastics. "Augustine is completely on our side" was Calvin's boast; he became the one figure who, more than any other, enabled the leaders of the Reformation to claim that they were not throwing over the Christian past after all. But more than any of these soloists of the Middle Ages, the Renaissance, and the Reformation, it was, as far as we can tell, the silent in the land, those who did not write and could not read, who took over elements of the Augustinian tradition and transformed them into that protean mass of practices and beliefs that historians now call the medieval tradition.

"Well, if it's a show about tradition and its dissolution, then the audience should be told what that tradition is": this statement of Jerome Robbins deserves to be raised to the status of what Immanuel Kant, in his definition of the categorical imperative, called "a maxim of universal law." The maxim applies above all to education, whose young audience should be told what that tradition is as part of the record of its dissolution. For even if—or especially if—the tradition of our past is a burden that the next generation must finally drop, it will not be able to drop it, or to understand why it must drop it, unless it has some sense of what its content is and of how and why it has persisted for so long. The tradition does not have to be understood to be dominant; as Czeslaw Milosz has observed, "Certainly, the illiterates of past centuries, then an enormous majority of mankind, knew little of the history of their respective countries and of their civilization," and yet their lives were decisively shaped by that history. In fact, so long as the tradition is not understood, some parts of it, however transmuted they may be, can continue to be dominant: we may no longer know what was meant by creation in the image of God, but most of the daily newspapers in the United States publish horoscopes.

Knowledge of the traditions that have shaped us, for good or ill or some of both, is not a sufficient preparation for the kind of future that will face our children and our grandchildren in the twenty-first century—not a sufficient preparation, but a necessary preparation. The rediscovery of tradition belongs to the design of the curriculum, and to the definition of the goals and the content of general education, also in a nation that has—if I may say so, traditionally—been more hungry for its future than addicted to its past. That rediscovery is made possible, and made necessary, by the continuity of tradition, what Edmund Burke called a "partnership in all science, all art, every virtue." But, Burke added, "As the ends of such a partnership cannot be obtained in many generations, it becomes a partnership not only between those who are living, but between those who are living, those who are dead, and those who are to be born." And that, come to think of it, is not a bad definition of living tradition.

TWO

The Recovery of Tradition

A Case Study

hroughout the discussion of tradition in my first lecture I have been careful to speak about *rediscovery*, not about *recovery*, for the two are by no means the same. There have been many, particularly in the nineteenth century and since, for whom the rediscovery and the critical study of a tradition that they had been affirming uncritically has led to the repudiation of that tradition, when for the first time they have recognized, with a shock, just what they had been reciting and doing. I recall staying at a Benedictine monastery shortly after the repeal of the law requiring that the daily office be recited in Latin. One elderly lay brother, who did not know much Latin but had been chanting the Psalter in Latin ever since his days as a novice, was now beginning to come to terms with the Psalms in English. During my stay, the community came to Psalm 137 (Psalm 136 in the Vulgate), whose Latin title is *Super flumina Babylonis*. It closes

with the verse: "Beatus, qui tenebit et allidet parvulos tuos ad petram!" which, being translated, means: "Happy shall be he who takes your little ones and dashes them against the rock!" When the poor old man understood fully what he had been asking the Almighty to do all these years, he was visibly shaken.

So it has frequently been in the past two centuries, as critical historical study has discovered and exposed the full story of many of our most cherished ideas and institutions. Rediscovery can often lead to rejection, and it will undoubtedly continue to do so; for even if "you can't go home again," it will not be what Czeslaw Milosz has called the "new obsession . . ., a refusal to remember," but a mature and critical rediscovery of the past, that will set you free from supposing that you do have to go home again. But I would be less than honest if I did not go on to say that for others, and for myself among them, the historical rediscovery of tradition has instead gone hand in hand with the existential recovery of tradition. For this recovery through rediscovery, no less than for repudiation through rediscovery, the nineteenth century supplies many of the most important paradigms.

Among these, none has been more important than John Henry Newman. It was Newman's rediscovery of tradition that led him, in 1845, to conclude that he could not consistently advocate its recovery and remain an Anglican, so that on 9 October 1845 he was received into the Roman Catholic Church. The specific form that his consideration of tradition had taken by 1845 is evident from his *Essay on the Development of Christian Doctrine* of that year. But as he tells us in his autobiographical *Apologia pro vita sua*, "Even at an earlier date I had introduced [the principle of development of doctrine within

tradition] into my History of the Arians in 1832." He is referring to what he himself would call his "first work," *The Arians
of the Fourth Century, Their Doctrine, Temper and Conduct, Chiefly
as Exhibited in the Councils of the Church between A.D. 325 and
A.D. 381,* published in 1833.

In his thoughtful biography of Newman, Louis Bouyer has
said:

> The publication of his *Arians of the Fourth Century* coincided with
> the start of the [Oxford] Movement. This work, for which he had
> relied on his own unaided resources, and which is somewhat
> suggestive of the prentice hand, is crammed with facts and
> citations from the ancient writers, all of them carefully digested
> and deeply pondered. But, more than that, there shines out,
> through the vision of the past which illumines it, his faith in a
> living Church. It is this belief in the existence of an ever living
> Catholic Church, reflected in the writings of Athanasius, Basil,
> Gregory, and the like, that it was now Newman's aim to define,
> so that he might reinfuse it into the Anglicanism of his day.

Having written recently, and at some considerable length,
both about Newman's *Essay on Development* and about his *Idea
of a University,* I want to turn here to *The Arians of the Fourth
Century* as a case study for the recovery of tradition, and to do
so on the basis of a close reading of this remarkable book, with
fairly extensive quotation, as befits a case study. For in it
Newman sets forth in detailed fashion both the process and
the implications of that recovery, in a way that has a significant
bearing on the entire enterprise to which we are giving our
consideration here in these lectures.

While the hero of the piece is clearly Athanasius, the patri-
arch of Alexandria, Newman came to feel that in the original
version of *The Arians of the Fourth Century* he had perhaps

exaggerated the individual heroism of this "father of orthodoxy." For in the third edition, published in 1871, he added
the footnote: "Justice has not been done here to the ground of
tradition, on which the Fathers specially took their stand"; and
in substantiation of this judgment he quoted Athanasius, who
saw in loyalty to tradition the most decisive difference between orthodoxy and heresy. That correction was, however,
quite in keeping with the basic scope of the original, in which
Newman had set his study of heresy and orthodoxy during the
fourth century into the context of the history of tradition in the
early church, interpreting the Council of Nicea and the trinitarian theology of Athanasius as the vindication of tradition; or,
as he would put it in the *Essay on Development*, "St Athanasius's
condemnation of [Arian] theology is a vindication of the Medi-
aeval." Newman's historic contributions both to the rediscovery of tradition and to the recovery of tradition are the
long-term outcome of the historical and theological research of
which *The Arians of the Fourth Century* was the firstfruits.

Although Newman stated his purpose in publishing *Arians*
as "historical and explanatory," without involving himself in
"controversy or proof," it is almost impossible to miss the
central point of the book, which may well be identified as one
of the pervading themes of Newman's thought about tradition: Newman was undertaking the vindication of tradition,
by using history to transcend antitheses and to hold together
principles that polemics on all sides had set into opposition.
The recovery of tradition enabled him to say "both/and" rather
than "either/or."

In the areas of thought with which Newman was dealing,
the most fundamental of these polemical antitheses was that
between the Bible and the church, which was transcended by

the discovery of a ground of apostolic tradition on which the church fathers had taken their stand. It was obvious to him that there had been "such tradition, granting that the Apostles conversed, and their friends had memories, like other men." Newman identified "the Apostolical Tradition" as "practically the chief source of instruction" in the "primitive age" of the church, and attributed to this tradition the advantage over the Scriptures that, "being withdrawn from public view, it could not be subjected to the degradation of a comparison [with the New Testament], on the part of inquirers and half-christians." This apostolic tradition was not a later accretion, as the Protestant Reformers had charged, but had been contemporary with the New Testament writings from the beginning. "A traditionary system of theology, consistent with, but independent of Scripture," had, according to Newman, "existed in the Church from the Apostolic age."

The central element in that system was the doctrine of the Trinity, which, though not formally adopted as a dogma until the Council of Nicea in 325, had been "given to the Church by tradition contemporaneously with those apostolic writings" of the New Testament and was only confirmed, not invented, at Nicea. But by the time of Nicea and afterward, which is the period Newman was describing in this book, "the line of tradition, drawn out as it was, to the distance of two centuries from the Apostles, had at length become of too frail a texture" to serve as an authority without being reduced to creedal formulas. It was that weakening of "the cogency of Apostolic Tradition" that necessitated "the imposition of doctrinal tests." There was, then, according to Newman's reading of history, a precreedal "traditionary system, received from the first age of the Church." Recognition of this "traditionary system" likewise made it possible for him to hold together not only the Bible and the church, or Scripture and tradition, but also an awareness of the limitations of creedal formulas and a recognition of their necessity: "imposing an authoritative creed" was a "novel, though necessary measure."

When the controversies over the relation between Father and Son in the Trinity had begun, not even the "traditional statements of the Catholic doctrine, which were more explicit than Scripture, had . . . taken the shape of formulae." The language of the early church fathers had been "for the most part as natural and unpremeditated" as that of the New Testament. Then, "either from Apostolical traditions, or from primitive writings," the church moved out of this traditionary system to its explicit and authoritative creeds. Newman recognized, on the one hand, that "there are no two opinions so contrary to each other, but some form of words may be found vague enough to comprehend them both"; and, on the other hand, that it was possible for two groups of Christian believers to be "agreeing in doctrine, though differing in the expression of it." He was prepared, he said, to "avow my belief, that freedom from symbols [i.e., creeds] and articles [of faith] is abstractedly the highest state of Christian communion, and the peculiar privilege of the primitive Church." He sought simultaneously to dissociate this uneasiness about "symbols and articles" from the liberalism of his own time, "that proud impatience of control in which many exult, as in a virtue," and to criticize the "timid and narrow-minded men" of the fourth century (and, presumably, not only of the fourth century) "who thought that orthodoxy consisted in being at all times careful to comprehend in one confession the whole of what is believed on any article of faith."

By contrast both with such hostility to authoritative dogma and with such eagerness to be explicit about everything possible (in Lewis Carroll's phrase, directed apparently against Newman's disciple W. G. Ward, to "believe as many as six impossible things before breakfast"), the tradition of orthodoxy, in Newman's reading, had always observed a reverent restraint. He referred to this as "an economical relinquishment of a sacred doctrine." It was once again from Athanasius that his ammunition came, in the form of an attack on those who "dare to speak flippantly on subjects too sacred to approach, mortals as they are, and incapable of explaining even God's works upon earth." Likewise from Athanasius he derived the methodology of affirmation by negation (often called *apophatic*, from the Greek word for "negation"), which he employed to go beyond the conventional alternatives. "We cannot understand" the divine essence, and yet "we know as much as this, that God exists," which was "the way in which Scripture speaks of Him." From Gregory Nazianzus, usually surnamed "the Theologian" because of his exposition and defense of the doctrine of the Trinity in his *Theological Orations* of 380, he quoted the axiom "Let the doctrine be honoured silently," and once again he used Athanasius as the authority to justify "the silence of the Apostles" and of the orthodox church on the content of the tradition.

The specific content of the apostolic tradition had remained secret because so much of it, in the precreedal "traditionary system, received from the first age of the Church," had been not dogmatic, but liturgical in its form. It was symptomatic of the loss of tradition in modern times, and of the need for its recovery, that now "we count the words of the Fathers, and measure their sentences; and so convert doxologies into

creeds." From the church fathers of the fourth century Newman knew that then "the public doxology . . . was practically
the test of faith." To use a distinction quoted in my first lecture,
the authentic tradition of orthodoxy was not a matter to be
decided by an intellectually formulated "rule of faith" set forth
by scholars and theologians, but by the "rule of prayer" of "the
thousand of silent believers, who worshipped in spirit and in
truth." For the seat of orthodoxy in the fourth century was
"the faith of uneducated men," which, Newman insisted, "is
not the less philosophically correct, nor less acceptable to God,
because it does not happen to be conceived in those precise
statements, which presuppose the action of the mind on its
own sentiments and notions." From the church fathers he
quoted the axiom "The ears of the common people are holier
than are the hearts of the priests." Tradition for Newman was,
therefore, a profoundly democratic concept, which did not
trickle down from theologians, popes, and councils to the
people, but filtered up from the faithful (who are the church) to
become the subject matter for the speculations, controversies,
and systems of the dogmatic theologians.

Despite what he had come to see now as a specious opposition between Scripture and tradition, it was, and continued to
be, "the chief office" of those early traditions to provide a
method of "interpreting and harmonizing the statements of
Scripture." Listing several such statements, which on their
face seemed to contradict one another, Newman described the
language of Scripture as "perplexed in the extreme" unless
one had the proper traditional "key." Such biblical language,
when put forward by heretics without that key from tradition,
was "of course inadequate to concentrate and ascertain the
true doctrine" of the Trinity. "Guidance from tradition" had

served to clarify for Catholic teaching in the third and fourth centuries what the Bible meant when it called Christ the "Son" of God.

Apparently there had also been in the church a secret "traditionary explanation" of many passages from the Old Testament that are not cited in the New Testament; Newman refers to the use of the sacrifice of Isaac by Abraham as a "type" of the sacrifice of Christ, but he could have referred as well to the recitation of the words "For unto us a child is born" as a prophecy of the birth of Christ even though the New Testament does not apply them in this way. For, as Newman was now quite sure, it had never been the purpose and function of Scripture "to *teach* us our creed"; the church did that out of its tradition, and then it would "appeal to Scripture in vindication of its own teaching." Nor was anyone to conclude from this "that this appeal to tradition in the slightest degree disparages the sovereign authority and sufficiency of holy Scripture, as a record of the truth." Tradition, according to an early father of the church, did not "supersede Scripture" as though "supplanting or perverting the inspired records"; rather, it was to be employed "in conjunction with Scripture" as "a corroborating, illustrating, and altogether subordinate tradition."

The secret and implicit tradition became public and explicit in the course of time and then "ceased to exist even in theory," as "it was authoritatively divulged, and perpetuated in the form of symbols according as the successive innovations of heretics called for its publication." Therefore the history of the emergence of these symbols was the consequence jointly of "the experience of controversy, and the voice of Tradition." But just as the experience of controversy and the voice of tradition were not antithetical, but complementary, so once

again it was essential to avoid setting into opposition two
principles that tradition had managed to hold together: hostility to innovation and readiness to employ new formulas that
did not appear in the Bible. It was the heretics who were guilty
of what Newman calls "successive innovations," relying as
they did "on their dialectical skill, and not on the testimony of
the early Church."

Nevertheless, when the Council of Nicea incorporated the
term *homoousion* ("one in being with the Father") into its creed,
that was not an innovation. For "the discharge of this office [of
imposing a creed] is the most momentous and fearful that can
come upon mortal man," Newman acknowledged; but that
was the "peculiar duty" of "the collective illuminations of
the Heads of the Church," who had been "appointed of the
Holy Ghost to be overseers of the Lord's flock." And so,
"when innovations arise, they must discharge it to the best of
their ability." That is what they did in promulgating the
homoousion when the "innovation" of Arianism arose. It
would, Newman insisted, have been "a superstition, an en-
croachment on Christian liberty, and an impediment to freedom of thought" to forbid this term on the grounds that it did
not appear in Scripture. This was especially so, he added
somewhat portentously, "considering that a traditionary system of theology, consistent with, but independent of Scripture
has existed in the Church from the Apostolic age."

The "statements" contained in that traditionary system,
"though not given to us as inspired, probably are derived from
inspired teachers." Certainly the content of the homoousion,
if not the term, belonged to the normative apostolic tradition,
according to Newman. Sometimes, in "one of those frustrat-
ing passages which from time to time baffle and trouble every

reader of Newman," he seems to imply that perhaps the word itself did as well. At the end of his lengthy excursus on it, he calls it "a word long known in the Church, *almost found in Scripture*, and less figurative and material in its meaning than any which could be selected, and objectionable only as used by heretics." The use of it by heretics had brought homoousion temporarily into disrepute, until orthodoxy rescued it—or, perhaps more accurately, reclaimed it—and made it "the sole practical bulwark of the Catholic faith against the misrepresentations of heresy." The same was true of another term in the Nicene Creed, the identification of the Son of God as "light from light"; although it was "the orthodox and *almost apostolic* emblem of the derivation of the Son from the Father," it had been subject to abuse by heretics, until the creed restored it to respectability.

The function of tradition, as that which made it possible for Newman to say "both/and" rather than "either/or" in all of the ways we have been examining, could be extended even to the relation between revealed theology and natural theology. Asserting as he did, in the case of the original Christian revelation, that it was not confined to the text of the New Testament but had existed alongside the New Testament in the form of an authentically apostolic tradition, Newman likewise affirmed that "we must confess, on the authority of the Bible itself, that *all* knowledge of religion is from Him, and not only that which the Bible has transmitted to us." On the basis of the Alexandrian theology of the second and third centuries, Newman called the content of such natural knowledge of God "the *Dispensation of Paganism.*" The form of that knowledge, however, was tradition, or, as Newman was prepared to call it (and in italics at that), "*the divinity of Traditionary Religion.*"

Newman, who had early been exposed to the *View of the Evidences of Christianity* by William Paley, "this clearheaded and almost mathematical observer," and who all his life acknowledged his great debt to Joseph Butler's *Analogy of Religion*, was nevertheless quite chary of making claims that "the phenomena of the visible world would in themselves have brought us to a knowledge of the Creator." Instead of relying on such conventional proofs for the existence of God as the Thomistic argument from cause or the argument from design, he found the starting point for his apologetic in the concept of tradition. The natural knowledge of God, he preferred to say, would have come from "the universal tradition of His existence . . . , graciously preceding the study of the evidence [from nature]," not from such study of the evidence directly and immediately. He rejected any suggestion that "the heathen literature itself had any direct connexion with the matter of Christianity." On the contrary, there were in paganism "the scattered fragments of those original traditions which might be made the means of introducing a student to the Christian system"; they were "the ore in which the true metal was found." One such ore was "the language of Platonism."

It was a universal phenomenon that there was "something true and divinely revealed, in every religion all over the earth, overloaded, as it may be, and at times even stifled by the impieties which the corrupt will and understanding of man have incorporated with it." Nevertheless, for example in the language of Platonism, "from very early times, traditions have been afloat through the world, attaching the notion of a Trinity, in some sense or other, to the First Cause," although it was "altogether doubtful" whether Plato himself had done so. And so it was possible to make the blanket assertion that "all men have had more or less the guidance of tradition." Although it may have been "very faint or defective," consequently, this universal tradition of the knowledge of God was valid, as far as it went. Therefore, in Newman's words, "revelation, properly speaking, is an universal, not a partial gift," and it was invalid to define "the distinction between the state of Israelites formerly and Christians now," on the one hand, "and that of the heathen," on the other hand, in such a way as to suppose "that we can, and they cannot attain to future blessedness."

The operative conclusion from this understanding of the relation between primitive tradition and Christian tradition was carried out in the missionary practice of the early church, as visible not only in the sermon of the apostle Paul to the Athenians, but in the way it addressed its gospel to its hearers everywhere. The church of the apostles and of the church fathers did not engage, as had the evangelical Anglicanism of Newman's youth, in "stimulating the affections (e.g., gratitude or remorse), by means of the doctrine of the atonement, in order to [bring about] the conversion of the hearers." Instead, the preaching of the primitive church as documented in the New Testament and a fortiori in the apologetics of its second-century interpreters had, as "its uniform method," chosen "to connect the gospel with natural religion, and to mark out obedience to the moral law as the ordinary means of attaining to a Christian faith." The point of contact between natural religion and revealed religion was not in the first instance natural reason, but natural tradition, to which revealed tradition attached itself.

As it was the recovery of the concept of tradition that enabled Newman to hold together the universality of natural

religion and the particularity of revealed religion, so it also
provided him with a means of relating the universal and the
particular within the history of revealed religion itself. For
despite the appeal of such church fathers as Irenaeus of Lyons
to "the clearness and cogency of the traditions preserved in
the Church" as though these traditions constituted a single
and total entity, what any student of early Christian literature,
including John Henry Newman, confronts in the sources is
usually what Newman calls "local tradition, which each separate Christian community already possessed." And it is prin-
cipally with such specific and local traditions that most of *The
Arians of the Fourth Century* deals. The title of the first chapter is
"Schools and Parties in and about the Ante-Nicene Church,
Considered in Their Relation to the Arian Heresy." These
included Antioch and Alexandria as local traditions. In the
case of the former Newman sought to identify "the historical
connexion . . . between the Arian party and the school of
Antioch," while in the case of the latter he endeavored to
prove that "though the [Arian] heresy openly commenced, it
but accidentally commenced in Alexandria." Tertullian served
as documentation for the "express" trinitarian orthodoxy of
"the Ante-Nicene African school."

Even while he was making that reference to Africa, however, Newman was particularly interested in "the Ante-
Nicene school of Rome." He observed that "the Roman Church
[was] even then celebrated for its vigilant, perhaps its over-
earnest exactness, in matters of doctrine and discipline" and
hence "was made the arbiter of the controversy" when other
patriarchal centers became involved in disputes. Moreover,
during the specific period that forms the subject matter of *The
Arians of the Fourth Century*, the age of Athanasius, "Rome was

the natural mediator between Alexandria and Antioch," whose "support" became "still more important" to Athanasius as a consequence. The first edition of *Arians* contained two passages referring to the modern Church of Rome as, respectively, "a corruption of Christianity" and "the Papal Apostacy." In the third edition of 1871, as the author explained, these "two sentences, which needlessly reflected on the modern Catholic Church, have, without hurting the context, been relegated to a place by themselves at the end of the Appendix."

For in the interim Newman had, of course, come to the conclusion that he could not carry out his recovery of tradition—or, as Bouyer calls it, his "belief in the existence of an ever-living Catholic Church"—by "reinfus[ing] it into the Anglicanism of his day": he had to follow the tradition where it led him, which was into the fellowship and the obedience of that very Roman Church. He had spoken already in the *Lectures on the Prophetical Office of the Church* of 1837 about the "Prophetical Tradition, existing primarily in the bosom of the Church itself." In his *Essay on the Development of Christian Doctrine* of 1845 he quoted these words of his, though with the note that they had been written originally "from a very different point of view from that which I am taking at present"; for they had now come to mean that the universal tradition he had been affirming was preserved and available only within the particularity of Roman Catholicism.

Despite his interest in the specific traditions of Antioch and of North Africa, or even in those of Alexandria and of Rome, Newman was concerned, both before his conversion of 1845 and after it, chiefly for this universal tradition. In fact, the very sentence from *Arians* about "local tradition" that I quoted earlier reads in full: "Moreover, it [the Council of Nicea in 325] had confirmed by the combined evidence of the universal Church, the argument from Scripture and local tradition, which each separate Christian community already possessed." There might be idiosyncrasies in one or another of those local Christian traditions, such as the propensity of "the Greeks [to manifest an] . . . instinctive anxiety for philosophical accuracy of expression," and that of "the Latins [to emphasize] . . . the popular and practical side of the doctrine." But to the extent that a local theology went beyond idiosyncrasy to a genuine divergence, it was no longer entitled to the honorific title of "tradition," as the case of Antiochene theology and "the detestable blasphemy" of Arianism demonstrated. In opposition to any such local and sectarian theology it was necessary to invoke the authority of universal Catholic tradition.

In reading this youthful work about tradition written by the nineteenth century's principal exponent of the recovery of tradition, it is probably irresistible to look for anticipations of his mature theories of tradition. There are at least two aspects of tradition to which Newman adverts in *The Arians of the Fourth Century* that were to become the topics of full-dress treatment in his later works. He opens his section entitled "Variations in the Ante-Nicene Theological Statements" with the observation: "There will, of course, be differences of opinion, in deciding how much of the ecclesiastical doctrine . . . was derived from direct Apostolical Tradition, and how much was the result of intuitive spiritual perception in Scripturally-informed and deeply religious minds." The relation between tradition and intuition, to which I shall return at the close of the next lecture, is an issue that was to recur in a book that has been characterized as "Newman's chief philosophical work,"

An Essay in Aid of a Grammar of Assent, which appeared in 1870. I cannot examine here the relation of Newman's ideas about intuition and "illative sense" in the *Grammar of Assent* to what Etienne Gilson, in his sprightly introduction for a modern edition of the work, calls the "purely patristic intellectual formation" that had shaped Newman's thought. But it does seem appropriate to say that in his espousal of intuition as a source of knowledge alongside tradition Newman was in fact following the lead of that purely patristic intellectual formation. Even when he refused to give tradition credit for everything, he was being loyal to tradition.

Far more striking is the lack of emphasis on the concept of development, despite Newman's statement in the *Apologia* that he "had introduced it into my History of the Arians in 1832." As Yves Congar observes, "with Newman—not that he was the only one, but he was and remains to this day the *locus classicus* for the question—the idea of development became an inner dimension of that of tradition." Over and over, a reader familiar with the *Essay on Development* will look here in *Arians* for that inner dimension, but usually in vain. Newman seems to have recognized this lacuna. In the concluding paragraph of his first chapter he acknowledged "that deeper and more interesting questions remain," including heresy's "relation towards the subsequently-developed corruptions of Christianity," but he explained that they were "too large to be imagined in the design of a work such as the present." He would return to them in the *Essay on Development*; and when he did, the subject matter of *Arians,* and sometimes its very words, were put into a new context, as, in Congar's phrase, tradition acquired its "inner dimension" in the idea of development.

Newman's *Arians of the Fourth Century* makes a good case

study both for the rediscovery of tradition and for the recovery of tradition, for it represents both Newman's original research into the history of tradition and his personal appropriation of it. For his own part, he wanted nothing to do with a scholarly and historical rediscovery of tradition that did not issue in such a recovery; "to be deep in history is to cease to be a Protestant," he was to say in the *Essay on Development*. By contrast, he was far more tolerant toward a recovery of tradition that was uninformed by historical scholarship, believing as he did in the soundness of "the faith of uneducated men," which was the body of the tradition. But he came to see, already here in *Arians*, that once this tradition had been lost, also among the "silent believers," its recovery was impossible without historical research. His century was the golden age of that research, but it was as well the golden age of the relativism or "historicism" that declared the tradition to be historically determined and hence undeserving of the kind of loyalty that Newman's recovery of it had generated. The relation between historicism and recovery will therefore have to concern us in the next lecture.

THREE
Tradition as History

An Apologia

 am not altogether certain that Thomas Jefferson would have approved of a series of lectures in his honor that bore the title "The Vindication of Tradition"—which is a nice way of saying that I am altogether certain that Mr. Jefferson would have disapproved. For tradition was to him chiefly a hindrance, not a help, in the enhancement of life, the protection of liberty, and the pursuit of happiness. As our premier historian of the American experience has observed,

> The Jeffersonian was not confined by any particular tradition: he had sought to reform the Christian tradition, he had disavowed the humanist tradition, and he had set himself outside the English tradition. The past, through which other men had discovered human possibilities, was for him corrupt and dead.

Nor would Martin Luther have found such a title to his liking. He referred contemptuously to what in his own language he called *Menschensatzungen*, "human traditions," which he contrasted with the pure and original message of the word of God, unencumbered by the human additions of the intervening centuries. Each in his own way, Jefferson and Luther were summoning their contemporaries to move beyond tradition or behind tradition to authenticity: Tradition was relative and had been conditioned by its history, Truth was absolute and had been preserved from historical corruption.

It was in the interest of documenting this contrast between authentic Truth, uncorrupted by history, and a historically relative tradition that both Luther's sixteenth century and Jefferson's eighteenth-nineteenth century made extensive use of the historical argument in controversy. The claim that the papacy had been divinely instituted and hence possessed supernatural authority was untenable, Luther and his colleagues charged, in the light of history, which showed that the institutions, the practices, and even the doctrines of the church had changed over centuries. "As it was in the beginning, is now, and ever shall be, world without end" applied to God and to the word of God, but not to the ever-mutable tradition of the church. Trained as many of them were in the critical methodology and "sacred philology" of Renaissance humanism, the Protestant Reformers helped to lay the foundations for historical research into the genesis and the evolution of cherished traditions that had come down from the Middle Ages and from the church fathers. By this research they exploded the assumption of a "consensus of the centuries," upon which the authority of tradition rested.

What the Reformation of the sixteenth century had done in its historical critique of the papacy or the sacraments or the legends of the saints, the Enlightenment of the eighteenth century did to many other sacred traditions, including some traditions that the mainstream of the Protestant Reformation had declared out of bounds for such destructive criticism (for example, the orthodox dogmas of the Trinity and of the divine and human natures in Christ). Inevitably, the very norms in the name of which the criticism of tradition had carried out its program came under historical-critical scrutiny themselves: "the laws of nature and of nature's God" (to use the phraseology of the Declaration of Independence), which by contrast with the welter of individual human laws were supposedly constant and self-evident, now showed themselves to be no less the product and the victim of historical change; and the Bible, too, had come into being, both as individual books and as a sacred canon, amid all the changes and chances of Near Eastern history over a period of a millennium and more.

Once it had been set free to do its work, the method of historical-critical study could not accept the notion of any privileged sanctuary to which it must not apply the same standards it was using elsewhere. As Sir Isaiah Berlin has noted, "The transformation of the writing of history in the nineteenth century is to a large degree the work of the great German masters from Niebuhr and Boeckh to Mommsen and Burckhardt, from Savigny and Ranke to Max Weber and Troeltsch." Through their work, the various areas of human experience, one by one, became objects of historical research, and the assumption grew that historical study of such an area of experience was the best means for comprehending it. Proceeding from the growing national consciousness of the age and nourishing that consciousness in turn, the historical study of each of the national literatures of the West established itself as the standard way of dealing with a text. Not its theme, nor its genre, but its place in the history of that literature, its genetic relation to the literary monuments preceding it and following it, and the specific historical circumstances of its author could "explain" the work. This made the determination of its authorship crucial to its interpretation, and the identification of the sources upon which it drew decisive for its place in the development of the literature.

The history of philosophical ideas had long been a component of doing philosophy; it is to Aristotle's interest in that history that we owe a considerable portion of what we know about the pre-Socratic philosophers. But now—first of all, of course, through Hegel, but then also through great classical scholars and later through great medievalists like Etienne Gilson—the evolution of philosophical systems took its place as the prolegomenon to the study of any future metaphysics. And the history of Christian doctrine, which had been a weapon in the hands of both sides during the Reformation debates, attracted scholars of various confessional backgrounds as a theological discipline unto itself. "The nineteenth century," as the most influential theologian of the twentieth century has commented somewhat ruefully, brought "the not altogether worthy spectacle of the escape of the very best theological minds into history"; they studied sources of dogma instead of writing systems of dogmatics.

Although such historical study sometimes fostered loyalty to a tradition and could even be responsible for the recovery of a tradition, as we have seen in the case of John Henry Newman, usually it carried on the earlier pattern of making the authority of tradition relative rather than absolute, by exposing its participation in the ebb and flow of historical currents. In response, the defenders of tradition often manifested a garrison mentality, seeking to demarcate those areas into which historical research, with its relativizing criticism, was not to be permitted to penetrate: first it was the Bible as such, then at any rate the New Testament, then at least the four Gospels, then ultimately the figure of Jesus Christ, that must be im- mune. Each such line of demarcation was, of course, no sooner drawn than crossed. The controversies at the end of the nine- teenth century over the critical study of tradition in theology were the most dramatic, with such defensive actions as the repression of Modernism within Roman Catholicism and the heresy trial of Charles Augustus Briggs by the General Assem- bly of the Presbyterian Church as points of battle. But I need only mention the earlier debates over the authenticity of the poems attributed to "Ossian," the acrimonious reactions pro and con to Lytton Strachey's *Eminent Victorians* of 1918, and in our own land and century the reviews and responses to Charles Beard's *Economic Interpretation of the Constitution* of 1913 as evidence that theologians and churchmen were not the only ones to find "historicism" (as the use of history to relativize tradition came to be known) a threat to the authority of cher- ished beliefs.

I may perhaps be permitted to observe that a two-edged sword does cut both ways: such a historical investigation as that of Friedrich Meinecke into the origins of historicism itself and into the ideas of its proponents leads to the conclusion that for many of them the rejection of the authority of tradition came first, and only then the discovery that tradition was historically relative (which was then used to justify the rejec- tion). Thus it is not historically fair to assign to historicism the exclusive credit (or blame) for undercutting tradition. The history of the historiography of the nineteenth century suggests, moreover, that there was a highly selective process of identifying those chapters from the total history of tradition that would most strikingly document the way the historical environment has molded the development of tradition and the way this development has therefore manifested constant change; the selectivity becomes visible, for example, in the table of contents of the often cited festschrift in honor of Shirley Jackson Case, dean of the Divinity School of the University of Chicago, entitled *Environmental Factors in Christian History*.

Meanwhile, the evidences for historical continuity, for what might be called the "nonenvironmental factors," have tended to receive far less attention in the scholarly literature. I have never seen it stated in print (except when I myself have stated it), and I am not quite sure just how I would go about documenting it, even with a string of footnotes. But it is, I think, a "self-evident truth" (if I may resort to a Jeffersonianism in this context) that, for more than nineteen centuries and in a great variety of cultures, Christians have been blessing bread and wine and celebrating the sacrament of the Eucharist nearly every day. If that is a self-evident truth, it is also a massive instance of continuity amid change, and a prime instance of the reality of tradition. It is as well the sort of phenomenon that the anthropologist, rather than the historian of ideas, would describe.

The historian of ideas would study, as indeed this historian of ideas has studied, the permutations of language and thought by which successive generations have sought to come to terms with the practice. Those permutations may truly be said to reflect change rather than chiefly continuity, as becomes obvious when the proponents of a particular theory of the eucharistic presence have sought to read it back into the texts of an earlier period. But the changes in theory were attempts to make sense of a continuing practice and, even in purely historical terms (whatever that may mean), do not themselves make sense apart from that continuing practice. But if the historian looks only at the changes of eucharistic theology, which is what most historians have done, the result will be a failure to do justice to the historical situation within which eucharistic theology has evolved—which has been a situation of continuity and hence of tradition.

The scholarly achievements of the historical-critical study of tradition during the nineteenth century are proof of its intellectual power. Where would any of us who work in intellectual history be, regardless of the period of our concentration, if it were not for the critical editions and scholarly monographs of historians who were inspired by the intense need to understand the development of traditions in their historical mise-en-scène? In my own discipline, all of us are perforce the beneficiaries of earlier monastic scribes and ecclesiastical compilers; you may recall Edward Gibbon's slightly grudging comment in the forty-seventh chapter of his *Decline and Fall* about the Abbé Tillemont: "And here I must take leave for ever of that incomparable guide—whose bigotry is overbalanced by the merits of erudition, diligence, veracity, and scrupulous minuteness." Yet there is no contesting the judgment that the critical historians of the past hundred years have more than matched all those ecclesiastical predecessors in the loving care they have expended on texts whose authority as part of normative tradition they no longer accepted.

When Karl Holl of the University of Berlin edited for the Berlin corpus of the Greek church fathers the complicated and lengthy text of the *Panarion* or *Refutation of All the Heresies* by the fourth-century heresiologist Epiphanius of Salamis, he tracked down the connections between Epiphanius and all the various books and fragments both of the heretics and of the heresy-hunters, through the labyrinthine ways of Byzantine literature. As his teacher and colleague, Adolf von Harnack, put it in his funeral address for Holl, he "applied to this task his incomparable capacity for work, his exquisitely reliable erudition, and his incorruptible critical judgment, thereby making this the very model of an edition of an ancient writer." Much of what Holl did with Epiphanius had never been done before and will never have to be done again. Yet he was not defending the authority of the kind of orthodoxy to which Epiphanius was so grimly dedicated. Dedicated Karl Holl unquestionably was, nevertheless, but to another tradition, the tradition of a historical research that would put the Byzantine tradition into context and would account for it on the basis of that context.

By this process the method and the results of the historical-critical study of tradition have themselves become tradition, which the entrenched critics of ancient traditions will defend with the same passion of commitment and the same apodictic sense of obvious truth that confronted historical-critical study when it first declared war on what Abraham Lincoln once called "the dogmas of the quiet past." Because the scholarship inspired by historicism has done its job so well, there is no going behind what is by now an ineradicable part of our own intellectual tradition. None of us can go back—and, I suppose, none of us would, except in an occasional wistful moment, want to go back—to a method of reading the traditions of our heritage that did not do justice to their historical character. Or, to put it more directly, none of us can ever again establish some sort of sanctuary into which the historical-critical study of "sacred tradition" may not enter. The history of thought, the history of science, and the history of faith are all filled with the "bare ruin'd choirs" of such sanctuaries.

Our task is, rather, to face the issue directly, and to do so as scholars and thinkers and citizens and believers (or, at any rate, as some of the above) who accept, gratefully or at least gracefully, all the historical disclosures that have come out of historicism and its research. And the unavoidable question is: How, then, may we acknowledge the human, all-too-human nature of the traditions that are our intellectual, moral, political, and spiritual heritage, and nevertheless (or perhaps even therefore?) affirm those traditions as normative and binding, and go so far as to call them, in some meaningful sense, sacred?

If the Constitution of the United States was, as we were told so frequently and so stridently in the 1960s, written by a group of "white male slaveholders"; if Israel came to the most overwhelming insight in human history, as expressed in the Shema, "Hear, O Israel, the Lord is our God, the Lord is one," not in the incandescent moment of the burning bush, but through centuries of evolution from the notion of a tribal deity to its eventual monotheism, for which it then created the traditions of the burning bush and of Sinai; and if the one, holy, catholic, and apostolic church began with a mistaken expectation of apocalypse, whose disappointment led to the appearance of tradition, liturgy, and dogma as a compensation—if, I say, any or all of these debatable hypotheses of the critical history of tradition may be said to have any truth to them, how may we who affirm as our own one or more of these traditions (not to say we who affirm all three of them) go on calling them a credo without whistling in the dark as we pass by the cemetery where history has buried tradition?

Having come just past the halfway point of these lectures, I should probably present whatever credentials I have for even taking up such questions. Beyond the temporary but heady sense of being an oracle that comes with the Jefferson Lectureship in the Humanities (a sense that my predecessors have resisted with greater or lesser success), I would urge that the very concept of tradition cannot be defined until a specific tradition has been studied at some depth, in the details of its concrete historical development. That is the case, I have been arguing, both with the rediscovery of tradition and with the recovery of tradition. Since the effort to make sense of the biblical message has the longest continuous development of any major intellectual movement in Western culture, the life-long scholarly study of it ought to provide some insights into the ways of tradition—not only of this tradition, in the case of my own scholarship the Christian tradition, but of any tradition so conceived and so dedicated.

At the same time, the texts, ideas, and institutions of the Christian tradition have also received closer scrutiny from the historical-critical method than those of all other traditions combined; for example, much of the methodology of modern textual criticism, whatever the text, is the product of the study of the manuscripts and versions of the New Testament, beginning with Erasmus and even earlier. It has likewise been the discovery of the relativities in the Christian tradition that has provided the historicism of the eighteenth and especially of the nineteenth century with its most detailed evidence, and in the thought of Ernst Troeltsch with its most provocative systematic statement. All of that gives me the responsibility, and I suppose the right, as a historian of the development of doctrine in the Christian tradition, to ponder the mystery of tradition—of its rediscovery and its recovery, of its history and its vindication.

To begin at the beginning, in fact with our own beginnings: tradition derives some of its vindication from the sheer fact of its existence, "just because it's there," as the cliché about mountain climbing says. Coming to terms with the presence of the traditions from which we are derived is, or should be, a fundamental part of the process of growing up. Obviously, that ought to include a knowledge of the contents of those traditions. As I have suggested earlier, we do not have a choice between being shaped by our intellectual and spiritual DNA and not being shaped by it, as though we had sprung into being by some kind of cultural spontaneous generation. Some teenagers (including certain teenagers well past their teens) seem to wear their clothes as though they had invented sex; yet their very presence here is an indication that someone must have thought of it before.

We do, nevertheless, have some choices to make. One, to which my first lecture was devoted, is whether to understand our origins in our tradition or merely to let that tradition work on us without our understanding it, in short, whether to be conscious participants or unconscious victims. Once understood, the tradition, unlike our biological DNA, does confront us with a further choice, discussed in my second lecture: the choice between recovery and rejection, with a range of possibilities that combine partial recovery with partial rejection. That choice, too, is real. But to base recovery on ignorance and implicit faith, as some previous generations have done, or to base rejection on ignorance and bigotry, as many in our own generation have done, is not worthy of a free and rational person. We do well to recognize as infantile an attitude toward our parents that regards them as all-wise or all-powerful and that is blind to their human foibles. But we must recognize no less that it is adolescent, once we have discovered those foibles, to deny our parents the respect and reverence that is their due for having been, under God, the means through which has come the only life we have.

Maturity in our relation to our parents consists in going beyond both a belief in their omniscience and a disdain for their weakness, to an understanding and a gratitude for their decisive part in that ongoing process in which now we, too, must take our place, as heirs and yet free. So it must be in our relation to our spiritual and intellectual parentage, our tradition. An abstract concept of parenthood is no substitute for our real parents, an abstract cosmopolitanism no substitute for our real traditions. Jerusalem truly is "the mother of us all," or perhaps more precisely the grandmother of us all, with Athens as our other grandmother (since everyone is entitled to two grandmothers). The tension and the complementarity between Athens and Jerusalem has been a recurring theme, a sort of melodic counterpoint, of our tradition. And it must still be, for us as descendants of those two grandmothers, with that melody that we learn to sing, and from that counterpoint that we go on to compose melodies of our own. To be tone-deaf to the tradition is, therefore, to be unable to hear the voices of the past or the present—or of the future.

It is, then, a mark of an authentic and living tradition that it points us beyond itself. To describe that quality of tradition, it may be helpful to invoke a distinction from tradition, specifically from the Eastern Christian tradition. In the course of the iconoclastic controversies, the vigorous debates of the eighth and ninth centuries over the propriety of the use of images, the distinction evolved between a token, an idol, and a true image or icon. An *idol* purports to be the embodiment of that which it represents, but it directs us to itself rather than beyond itself; idolatry, therefore, is the failure to pay attention to the transcendent reality beyond the representation. A *token*, on the other hand, does point us beyond itself, but it is an altogether accidental representation that does not embody what it represents. An authentic image, which came to be called *icon* in Greek and then in other languages, is what it represents; nevertheless, it bids us look at it, but through it and beyond it, to that living reality of which it is an embodiment. Applied to the question of how we may respect a tradition about which historical research has disclosed the embarrassing "true story," this distinction, which is I grant a bit abstract (it is, after all, the product of Greek thought and language), serves to identify a characteristic of genuine tradition that makes it a kind of icon and that sets it apart from tradition falsely conceived.

An idol, I said, purports to be the embodiment of that which it represents, but it directs us to itself rather than beyond itself. Tradition becomes an idol, accordingly, when it makes the preservation and the repetition of the past an end in itself; it claims to have the transcendent reality and truth captive and encapsulated in that past, and it requires an idolatrous submission to the authority of tradition, since truth would not dare to appear outside it. Such was the conception of the authority of tradition that Luther and the Reformation, but then even more Jefferson and the Enlightenment, perceived (whether accurately or inaccurately) in medieval thought, and against which they protested.

What the Enlightenment tended to substitute for it was the

definition of tradition as a token, a purely arbitrary representation that does not embody what it represents. The universal truths and values in the name of which Jefferson and the Enlightenment defied the idolatry of tradition did not depend for their validity on any of the specific traditions, whether of Jerusalem or of Athens. Hence it was not essential to cultivate and transmit those traditions once the universal values had been achieved; they were, to use a metaphor familiar from the history of mysticism, the ladder which one climbed to reach the window, but which one no longer needed once the window of universal truth was open. That view of tradition seems to assume, however, that the tradition will not be replaced by something far worse, and that the universal truths and values, once attained, no longer need the tradition to sustain them— an assumption for which the history of the past two centuries does not provide any great measure of reassurance. For, as Clifford Geertz has pointed out, "It is, in fact, precisely at the point at which a political system begins to free itself from the immediate governance of received traditions . . . that formal ideologies tend first to emerge and take hold."

Tradition qualifies as an icon, by contrast with both of the other views, when it does not present itself as coextensive with the truth it teaches, but does present itself as the way that we who are its heirs must follow if we are to go beyond it—through it, but beyond it—to a universal truth that is available only in a particular embodiment, as life itself is available to each of us only in a particular set of parents. Athens and Jerusalem are both human cities. Neither of them is, as such, the City of God "undimmed by human tears," that *civitas Dei* of which Augustine, and before him the seers of the Bible as well as Plato, all caught a vision. Yet it is to the traditions of Athens and

Jerusalem that their spiritual descendants must turn, over and over again—not to linger there permanently, but to find there, for each generation of descendants, what we for our part shall not recognize elsewhere (though it certainly is elsewhere, if God is one, as the Shema of Judaism and the Nicene Creed of Christian orthodoxy confess) unless we have first seen it here. That is how tradition as an icon sets itself apart from both the idol and the mere token. In so doing, it vindicates itself by managing to be as universal as the theorists of the token rightly insist that it must be, and yet at the same time as particular as the devotees of the idol correctly sense that it should be. But it refuses to choose between the false alternatives of universal and particular, knowing that an authentic icon, a living tradition, must be both.

Such an apologia for tradition as history, or at any rate for the history of the tradition of which we are the heirs, is not a lame excuse, thought up on the morning after the debacle of tradition. It is, rather, a summary, a restatement, and a recovery of some of the deepest elements in the tradition itself. Whatever each of them may mean for his special disciples, Moses, Socrates, and Jesus have been linked so often throughout most of the history of the tradition that we must see in them the primary source and chief inspiration for the very critique of a tradition that presumes to speak for them. Moses smashed the tablets of the divine law itself in protest against idolatry; Socrates was executed as an enemy of the tradition because he believed that "an unexamined life is not worth living" and an unexamined tradition not worth following; and Jesus went to the cross because he would not have any earthly form of the divine (not even, let it be remembered, his own) become a substitute for the ultimate reality of the living God.

Therefore no criticism of the tradition that was voiced by the evangelicalism of the Reformation or the rationalism of the Enlightenment or the historicism of the nineteenth century can ever match, for severity and power, the criticism that came from these, its noblest products and its most profound interpreters. Tradition has the right to vindicate itself by appropriating much of what its critics say, for it was said, not only against the tradition but within the tradition, long before.

The presence and the power, within the tradition, of such voices as these may suggest another mark by which to identify a living tradition: its capacity to develop while still maintaining its identity and continuity. There is an analogy, susceptible of oversimplification as all analogies are and yet profound and accurate, between the American-Constitutional tradition and the Judeo-Christian tradition in their manifestation of that capacity. The analogy first came to my attention when I heard my late colleague from the Yale Law School, Alexander Bickel, speaking about "development of doctrine"—a technical term that was, I am quite sure, invented in its modern sense by John Henry Newman in his *Essay on Development*, discussed in my preceding lecture.

In both traditions there is an authoritative and, by now, quite ancient text, by which the tradition is said to be "constituted" (hence the name "Constitution"). Membership in the community of each tradition comes through allegiance to that constitutive text, and holding office through a specific oath of allegiance. Such an oath upon taking office is required also from those whose task it will then be to interpret that text for situations and needs unforeseen in the explicit words of the text. The Supreme Court or a sanhedrin or an ecumenical council of the church must subordinate itself to the ancient authority even as it proceeds to decide what the authority means now; significantly, the promulgation of the dogma of papal infallibility by the First Vatican Council on 18 July 1870 specified that the pope was infallible "when he functions in his office as the pastor and teacher of all Christians," that is, as the spokesman for the deposit of faith in Scripture and tradition. In carrying out the task of interpretation, the supreme judiciary of church or state affirms the presumptive validity of decisions that have been made by its predecessors during the history of the community and its tradition. But this affirmation does not preclude, it rather presupposes that there must be, further "development of doctrine," to which, far more than to the mechanism of constitutional amendment or of dogmatic definition, the community looks for guidance that will recognize change but preserve continuity.

There will, of course, be unremitting controversy about the correct direction, proper rate, and apposite formulation of the development of doctrine; it is such controversy that provides employment for scholars of constitutional law, and, for that matter, historians of the development of Christian doctrine. But the demonstrated ability to sustain and eventually to accept the development of doctrine is witness to the vitality of a tradition. There is a kind of historical relativism that will emphasize only the variety of opinions and the irresistibility of change over the years, but will ignore the continuity. There is also a kind of strict constructionism that proceeds as though development were not real and were only the application of an unchanging and unchangeable authority to outward change. The American republic, the Jewish community, and the Christian church have all had advocates of both these interpretations, and they still do. But their accumulated wisdom has taught them to recognize—and the critical-historical study of their traditions has compelled them to acknowledge—that development is real but that it goes on within the limits of identity, which the tradition defines and continues to redefine. Like any growth, development may be healthy or it may be malignant; discerning the difference between these two kinds of growth requires constant research into the pathology of traditions. But it is healthy development that keeps a tradition both out of the cancer ward and out of the fossil museum.

Ultimately, however, tradition will be vindicated for us, for each of us as an individual and for us as communities, by how it manages to accord with our own deepest intuitions and highest aspirations (intuitions and aspirations which, if I am right in what I have been saying, are themselves imbedded in the tradition). Those intuitions and aspirations tell us that there must be a way of holding together what the vicissitudes of our experience have driven apart—our realism about a fallen world and our hope for what the world may still become, our private integrity and our public duty, our hunger for community and our yearning for personal fulfillment, what Pascal called "the grandeur and the misery" of our common humanity.

Earlier in this century, an English writer who knew how to be serious without becoming solemn, and clever without becoming silly, described his own experience of bringing these intuitions and aspirations together:

> And then followed an experience impossible to describe. It was as if I had been blundering about since my birth with two huge and unmanageable machines—the world and the . . . tradition. . . . When once . . . these two machines had come together, one after another, all the other parts fitted and fell in

with an eerie exactitude. I could hear bolt after bolt over all the machinery falling into its place with a kind of click of relief. Having got one part right, all the other parts were repeating that rectitude, as clock after clock strikes noon. Instinct after instinct was answered by doctrine after doctrine. Or, to vary the metaphor, I was like one who had advanced into a hostile country to take one high fortress. And when that fort had fallen the whole country surrendered and turned solid behind me. The whole land was lit up, as it were, back to the first fields of my childhood.

What did this for him was the vindication of tradition, defined, in his phrase, as "democracy extended through time . . . the democracy of the dead." It meant appealing from the tradition that Jefferson and Luther had rejected to the tradition that made both of them possible, a tradition in which, therefore, they too finally take their places of honor. And so perhaps it is not so incongruous after all, in a series of lectures named for Thomas Jefferson, the founder of our common tradition, to affirm and celebrate tradition as "the democracy of the dead," a "democracy extended through time" and through space.

FOUR

Tradition as Heritage

A Vindication

radition is the living faith of the dead, traditionalism is the dead faith of the living. And, I suppose I should add, it is traditionalism that gives tradition such a bad name. The reformers of every age, whether political or religious or literary, have protested against the tyranny of the dead, and in doing so have called for innovation and insight in place of tradition. In his first book, *Nature*, published in 1836, Ralph Waldo Emerson put their protest and their call into one question: "Why should not we have a poetry and philosophy of insight and not of tradition?"

What Emerson meant by "insight," moreover, especially in those early years, was the inner wisdom already present, always present, in the human spirit, over which the tyrants, whether of church or of state, must not cast the pall of an authoritarian past. Not as the transmitter of a received body of wisdom in the tradition, but as (in the words of his sensational

"Divinity School Address" of 15 July 1838) a "newborn bard of the Holy Ghost," the expositor of that "poetry and philosophy of insight" could set people free by helping them to cast away what I have called "the dead faith of the living," which is my definition of *traditionalism*, but was Emerson's definition of *tradition*. And in his Phi Beta Kappa address of 31 August 1837, "The American Scholar," which Oliver Wendell Holmes called "our intellectual Declaration of Independence," Emerson called upon the thinkers and scholars of the New World to throw off the last vestiges of spiritual and intellectual colonialism and to find their own authentic voice: "Why," indeed, "should not we have a poetry and philosophy of insight and not of tradition?"

There was, and is, evidence aplenty of the deadly effect that tradition has had on insight, especially in "poetry and philosophy" and in religion (which was, for Emerson, inseparable from poetry and philosophy). Even in periods of history that we now think of as times when innovation and creativity were bursting forth after a long winter, traditionalism could appear, dressed in the guise of a break with tradition. Jacob Burckhardt describes for us the process by which, in an effort to shake off what was regarded as the barbaric Latinity of Thomas Aquinas and the scholastics, "the consoling conclusion was at last reached, that in Cicero alone was the perfect model to be found. . . . Longolius, at Bembo's advice, determined to read nothing but Cicero for five years long, and finally took an oath to use no word which did not occur in this author."

Roman Catholicism had its Galileo, and Protestantism its Darwin, as prime instances of what Andrew Dickson White called "the warfare of science with theology." The recurring irony of that warfare, in which theologians resisted scientific innovation in defense of what they regarded as the established tradition of the faith, was that the tradition they were defending had in a previous age, and often a quite recent age at that, made its peace after controversy with a scientific hypothesis it had originally dismissed as inimical to the faith—and had done so, moreover, just when the scientific hypothesis itself was in the process of being superseded. Similarly, the perennial warnings of theologians about philosophical speculation as an activity dangerous to sound doctrine invariably come in the name of a "sound doctrine" that was the product of speculation and that has incorporated elements of some other philosophical perspective. The philosophers, in turn, have been capable of an intransigence that matched the dogmatism of the church even without the dogma of the church. It was, after all, as champions of an entrenched tradition that the nineteenth-century Hegelians of Denmark excommunicated a philosophical upstart named Søren Kierkegaard. It is only necessary to read the early chapters in the biographies of decisive men and women from any area of human endeavor to find examples aplenty of Emerson's antithesis between a poetry and philosophy of insight and the poetry and philosophy of tradition.

It is, indeed, from the history of human creativity in thought and in the arts that many of the horror stories about the sterility of tradition have come. Because the history of Christian dogma is usually thought to contain more such horror stories than all the rest of our history combined, scholarship in this field, as I have pointed out in my third lecture, was often in the advance guard of the battle against the authority of tradition. That scholarship was obliged, in the first instance, to justify its own enterprise, which was the application, to creed and dogma and sacred text, of the same criteria and methods of research that were appropriate to the other fields of the humanities. That is itself a slanted way of putting the matter, since the very point of much of the controversy was whether or not the history of the Christian tradition was a part of the humanities, so that it was legitimate to study the sacred tradition of dogma and even of Scripture in the same way as earlier Greek and Latin writings.

Christian theology, at any rate in its Eastern Orthodox and Roman Catholic configurations, has also been the one system of thought in which the concept of tradition is *ex professo* a chapter in the prolegomena to any statement of doctrine. Yet if the assumption is correct that we may and must study the history of dogma as we do the history of ideas generally, that *Dogmengeschichte* is part of *Geistesgeschichte*—and it is an assumption on which I have staked a lifetime of research and teaching—then the converse would seem to follow, as suggested earlier: the history of the concept of tradition in dogma ought to yield insight into the concept of tradition as such.

As I have maintained in my formulation of the analogy between the American-Constitutional tradition and the Judeo-Christian tradition, however, tradition, albeit under the nom de plume *precedent*, has played a similar role in the history of jurisprudence. During much of their history, notably in medieval thought, jurisprudence and theology have dealt with the concept of tradition in close collaboration. Medieval scholars like Ivo of Chartres took up the task of clarifying the authority of tradition, legal as well as theological, as the contradictions within a supposedly homogeneous body of teaching were becoming too conspicuous to ignore. The techniques for coping with those contradictions in the law, both civil law and canon law, helped to shape the development of a dialectical method of handling the juxtaposition of "Yes" and "No" (to use the title of Peter Abelard's famous book on the subject, *Sic et Non*) in Christian theology and ethics. Scholars were conscious of the limitations of the parallelism between these several traditions: civil law was easier to deal with in a critical and even in a historical way than was canon law, which was in turn less dangerous an arena for dialectic than was dogma, as Abelard himself and others after him were to learn.

Although the history of church dogma does probably provide the most generous supply of anecdotes about the tyranny of tradition over insight, some of them extremely dramatic, our own century has witnessed the confrontation between tradition and creativity at its most dramatic in the arts. Now that ballet has finally established itself across this entire nation, much of it quite traditional to be sure, a new generation may need the reminder of the shock to tradition that was delivered through ballet in the creations of Igor Stravinsky. To read again the accounts of Nijinsky by his adoring wife, the biography of Sergei Pavlovich Diaghilev, and above all the documents surrounding the premiere of *The Rite of Spring* on 29 May 1913, especially the rambling but delightful reminiscences of Stravinsky himself, is to have a box seat (or perhaps a loge) at what may well be the classic encounter between innovation and tradition.

Acknowledging that "strange as it may seem . . . , I was unprepared for the explosion myself," Stravinsky recalled many years later:

> Mild protests against the music could be heard from the very beginning of the performance. Then, when the curtain opened on the group of knock-kneed and long-braided Lolitas jumping up and down (Danse des adolescents), the storm broke. . . . The

uproar continued, however, and a few minutes later I left the hall in a rage; I was sitting on the right near the orchestra, and I remember slamming the door. I have never again been that angry. The music was so familiar to me; I loved it, and I could not understand why people who had not yet heard it wanted to protest in advance. I arrived in a fury backstage, where I saw Diaghilev flicking the house lights in a last effort to quiet the hall. For the rest of the performance I stood in the wings behind Nijinsky holding the tails of his *frac*, while he stood on a chair shouting numbers [in polysyllabic Russian] to the dancers, like a coxswain.

Beyond the sheer raw vitality of *Le Sacre du printemps*, which I am sure it will never quite lose, it was clearly the challenge to established musical tradition that precipitated the riot on that Paris night in May. Only the most unsophisticated in the audience could have been unaware of the constant change through which style had passed in the history of music since the Renaissance; but that change was evolution, and this change was revolution. In an evolutionary continuum, *tradition* can mean everything up to and including the latest stage in the process, so that the next and newest stage, while perhaps not exactly welcome, need not be any more of a threat than is the next and newest generation—which is, God knows, often threat enough. If that next generation of composers will only burn its pinch of incense at the shrine of the tradition, it will have the possibility, though not the guarantee, of a safe conduct as it moves on into new territory. But tradition demands to be served even when it is not observed. The dichotomy between insight and tradition, as stated by Emerson in the question I have quoted from *Nature*, has been a recurring theme in the life of the mind and spirit, so much so that one would be easily tempted to generalize it into a universal principle. As I shall be arguing at some length for the balance of this lecture, that temptation to superimpose our own antitheses on our history is a dangerous one. Nevertheless, the persistence of the issue across such a wide range of activities, intellectual and artistic and above all religious, does suggest the presence of something abidingly valid about it.

"The letter killeth, but the spirit giveth life," according to the primary authority of the Christian tradition. But the most profound expositors of the distinction between the letter and the spirit, from Origen in the third century and Augustine in the fifth to Thomas Aquinas in the thirteenth century and Martin Luther in the sixteenth, have all recognized, albeit with varying degrees of thoroughness and consistency, that it did not imply the elimination of the letter in favor of an exclusive concentration on the spirit. Rather, the interpreter was to begin with the letter, but must not stop there. When Augustine composed his *De Genesi ad literam* ("On the Book of Genesis according to the Letter"), he did seek to establish the literal sense of the text, or at any rate as much of the literal sense as an ignorance of Hebrew and an uneven knowledge of Greek would permit him to establish. But interpreting the story (or, rather, stories) of the creation in Genesis *ad literam* did not, apparently, include the necessity to teach that God made the world in six days of twenty-four hours each. Instead, Augustine posited an instantaneous creation. Thomas Aquinas, who preferred to take the "days" in Genesis as normal days, would not hereticize Augustine for this.

In relation to the controversies of the nineteenth and twentieth centuries, therefore, we may observe that the most influential biblical interpreter in the tradition of the Latin West knew what it meant to be *literal* without becoming *literalistic*—a distinction of which my own distinction at the beginning of this lecture between tradition as the living faith of the dead and traditionalism as the dead faith of the living may be seen as simply a corollary. But while Augustine may have known the distinction between literal and literalistic, even he did not always apply it; witness his fateful exegesis of the words of the Vulgate, "in whom [viz., in Adam] all have sinned," as the New Testament proof text for the doctrine of original sin. His epigones have often been far less aware of the distinction.

Thus the history of the Christian tradition is also the history of the critical reexamination of the tradition that has been made obligatory not by the inner dynamic of the tradition itself, but by the outsiders who have raised questions about the unexamined assumptions in the tradition: the heirs of Jerusalem (which in the preceding lecture I have called grandmother of the church), who looked at the same sacred text through a different set of spectacles; the heirs of Athens (which I have called the other grandmother of the church), who have been obliged to remind the custodians of the Christian tradition that the God who gave the tradition also made the human mind as the image of God, so that the tradition must be the object of thought no less than the object of faith; and, "as born out of due time," the critical historians, who have taken the Christian gospel literally in its insistence that it be studied historically and who have therefore investigated the tradition in its historical mutations through time. Yet these outsiders have, as often as not, been in some sense insiders at the same time. For (to stay with the language of Emerson, who was both an insider and an outsider, perhaps in that chronological order), the recognition of the tension between tradition and insight is itself an ineradicable element of the tradition itself, which must therefore not be identified with a traditionalism that seeks to preserve it by enbalming it.

Yet to say all of that and to say no more would be to do a serious historical injustice to the nature and the role of tradition in relation to insight. For during much of our history, insight has often come through the recitation and rearrangement of materials from tradition. I still remember when, almost forty years ago, I took up for the first time the study of a Byzantine literary genre known as the *florilegium* or "bouquet." This one was called *Doctrina patrum de incarnatione Verbi* ("Doctrine of the Fathers concerning the Incarnation of the Word"), although that is, of course, a Western and Latin title for an Eastern and Greek work. Unlike most other florilegia, it was available in a competent modern edition, by the Roman Catholic patristic scholar Franz Diekamp, published in 1907.

Trained as I was, as an heir of the scholarly tradition of the nineteenth century, to look for what an author's own "real position" was as distinct from the ritualistic repetition of the standard formulas, I skimmed through the quotations, for I was impatient to get to the author's own words. Then suddenly I was at the end of the treatise. There were few if any "author's own words," and hence apparently no "author's 'real position.'" There was only this seemingly random compilation of passages from various sources (which, in this case at least, the editor Diekamp had tracked down and identified for us). But the procedure by which I was accustomed to work in interpreting a Greek or Latin text could not satisfactorily address this genre of text, and it was only much later that I learned to follow another procedure.

What I learned, thanks to several Russian and Czech Byzantinists who became my mentors long after the completion of my formal studies (above all, the late Georges V. Florovsky), was that a florilegium was an explicit refusal to be "original," and that its originality and creativity must therefore be sought in its repetition of the standard formulas, not apart from that repetition. Hence the method of studying such florilegia is to lay several of them side by side; to note which passages from earlier sources appear in more than one of them; to compare these quotations to see if they are quoted identically, even if not accurately; to note which quotations appear in only one collection; and, finally, to examine and to try to understand the order of the arrangement itself.

For a florilegium is, I have come to think, like a ransom note sent by a kidnapper. The identification of the newspapers from which the individual words and letters have been clipped may become a clue to the date of the note and to the where-abouts and habits of the kidnapper, but it is in the arrangement of the clippings, whatever their sources, that the meaning of the document lies. Underlying my inability to discern that meaning in the *Doctrina patrum* was a false understanding of the relation between tradition and creativity, the assumption that the second began where the first left off. For to use a more genteel (and somewhat more Byzantine) figure of speech than that of the ransom note, a florilegium is a mosaic, all of whose tiles have come from somewhere else; a myopic examination of the tiles, or of the spaces between the tiles, misses the whole point, which is in the relation of the tiles to one another and of the mosaic to other mosaics.

Not even in Byzantium, however, were florilegia the only way of presenting the tradition. A more subtle, more "crea-tive" scheme for choreographing the doctors and thinkers of the past was to begin with a recital, but to interpolate into it statements about the current issue that were logically—and even syntactically—connected to the familiar quotations from the church fathers and church councils. Sometimes this seems to have involved the disingenuous attempt to pass off the addition as part of the original, and the instances of forgery, even by prominent and saintly figures, are too frequent to be dismissed. To be sure, a modern scholar does have to be careful about crying "Forgery!" prematurely, for there are occasions when Byzantine or medieval Western writers simply had access to more complete texts than we do. But it is noteworthy that modern scholars have been skillful and successful in identifying the instances of such forgery more often than they have been sensitive in penetrating to the method of handling tradition in relation to the topic of the hour as that method was at work in these amplified recitations of the received wisdom. I am thinking specifically of some of the *Acts* of Eastern church councils, but also of the works of individual Greek and Latin writers.

That method of handling tradition consisted in recital as a way of identifying what had not been said, but had been assumed, in the sources—or of what had not been said, but had been implied. Moving back to an assumption or forward to an implication became possible only by reciting the authoritative statement and then, so to speak, "teasing" the unspoken meaning out of it. In a similar vein, Alfred North Whitehead speaks in *Science and the Modern World* about how to discern what he calls "the philosophy of an epoch," namely, not by chiefly directing "your attention to those intellectual systems which its exponents feel it necessary explicitly to defend," but rather by finding "some fundamental assumptions which adherents of all the variant systems within the epoch unconsciously presuppose," assumptions that "appear so obvious that people do not know what they are assuming because no other way of putting things has ever occurred to them." In Byzantine thought, as well as in Western thought during the Middle Ages, a controversy over the tradition often provided the occasion for asking the documents of the tradition to yield those "fundamental assumptions" or to produce necessary implications for a question to which they had not been addressed. The condescending attitude of many modern interpreters toward such recitation, which often includes a stated preference for what is called "understanding," fails to recognize that during most of intellectual history understanding has come through reciting, or, to recur to the Emersonian antinomy, that insight was achieved by means of tradition.

Related to that method of teasing out the assumptions and implications from the tradition by reciting its received formulas was an even more profound, and even more precarious, technique. Not only did the formulas of the tradition contain assumptions that could now be spelled out, as well as implications that could now be drawn out; the formulas also were themselves specific instances of universal principles that could now be creatively reapplied to new situations. Some of the decisions of the Supreme Court seem, at least to a scholar who usually pores over other *constitutiones*, to involve some such technique. Certainly the framers of the Constitution of the United States had certain fundamental assumptions, not all of them stated in that document, which we today may, or perhaps must, state. Almost as certainly, what they did state in the articles may, by extension or extrapolation, be applied to situations created by modern technology or modern society which the framers could not have foreseen. But beyond the assumptions they did know and state elsewhere and the implications they did not know or state anywhere, there lie universal principles, as about the relation of the individual to society, about the relation of necessity to free will, or about the relation between distributive and retributive justice. To find these, it is not always possible to have recourse to the writings of Thomas Jefferson or the *Federalist* papers or the debates of the Continental Congress. Rather, scholars and jurists have looked to John Locke, to Aristotle, sometimes even to Robert Bellarmine, for such general principles, which may now give us guidance in a new world.

In the texts with which I am more familiar, such an identification of the general principles in the tradition has consisted very often in the clarification of the Platonism out of which the fathers and founders of the tradition have spoken. This Platonism lay behind the theological assumptions that the fathers did know and state elsewhere, as well as behind the theological and ethical implications that they did not know or state anywhere. For example, as I have mentioned in my third lecture, it became necessary in the eighth and ninth centuries to defend the use of icons in the church. In that defense there was some attempt to locate hidden theological assumptions and necessary theological and liturgical implications within the tradition. But what carried the day—in addition to the dramatic changes of political fortune represented by the accession of the empress Irene as regent in 780, and again by that of the empress Theodora in 842—was a method that moved from the writings of the great Cappadocian fathers of the fourth century (Basil of Caesarea, Gregory of Nyssa, and Gregory Nazianzus) to the universal principles of their Christianized Neoplatonism.

One of the most important of these principles was, of course, the relation between the particulars of sense-experience and the universal Forms. That principle, applied to the images by means of the analogy of the incarnation, justified the images in a situation where the explicit evidence of the tradition, and whatever that evidence seemed to assume or imply, seemed to oppose them. Conversely, where there has been a shift in philosophical universal principles, as for example between Augustine and Aquinas, this method of treating the tradition consisted in rescuing the valid doctrine of the tradition from the unfortunate metaphysical alliances it had formed, simultaneously preserving loyalty to the tradition and intellectual integrity.

Akin to these assumptions, implications, and universal principles, but broader in their application, are some other motifs from the tradition which, far from dampening or crushing the creative impulse, have served as sources of depth and power for it. For during much of our history, and down to our own time, tradition has provided the perennial themes and the key metaphors by which creative expression has been preserved from the banality and the trivialization to which a total immersion in the here and now could have subjected it. Eugene Genovese's *Roll, Jordan, Roll* is a rich and multi-layered account of how the metaphors of the Hebrew tradition, above all the biblical accounts of the captivity of Israel in Egypt and of the Exodus, have shaped the interpretation of the Black experience in America, sometimes by helping to make it bearable and sometimes by making clear just how unbearable it was.

Similarly, historians and philosophers of science have begun to describe for us the decisive role of root metaphors and paradigms in the creation of a *Weltbild*: which metaphors are chosen, and which tradition they come from, will profoundly affect the image of reality. Many such metaphors have in fact come from that borderland between orthodox Western theology and magic that we call the hermetic tradition, as researches into Kepler and even Isaac Newton have shown. As the positivistic and simplistic definitions of the scientific method that used to dominate the literature, though not the practice, of science have begun to yield to the recognition that a scientific discovery is in many ways akin to an aesthetic description of reality, there has also come a deepening awareness that in the history of science the relation between tradition and progress has been far more complex than the familiar anecdotes from the controversies over Galileo and Darwin would indicate. *Pace* both Ralph Waldo Emerson and Andrew Dickson White, tradition has been a source of insight as well as of warfare in that history.

In the aesthetic realm itself we have some of the most important evidence for this role of tradition as the source of persistent images that have fired the imagination and given form to the artistic vision. The suppression of the creative impulse by traditionalism is no more than half the story, and probably much less. Anyone who supposes that tradition must inhibit creativity need only listen, one after another, to two or three settings of the Mass, to hear how the composer has been able to find—Beethoven's *Missa Solemnis* in the "Kyrie," but Bach's *B-Minor Mass* in the "Dona nobis pacem"—a vehicle for an utterly personal and subjective voice in this eminently public and thoroughly traditional text of the Latin Mass. So idiosyncratic is each of them that some superficial interpreters have been tempted to dismiss the common element in all of them, which is the text of the Mass, as no more than a pretext which allowed the composers to say what they would have said anyway, since, after all, that text was "merely traditional." But tradition is not so "mere" as all that, even when the Mass is composed by Mozart the Catholic Freemason or Bach the orthodox Lutheran or Beethoven the believer/unbeliever. What deserves the description as "mere" is an artistic creativity that has undergone a frontal lobotomy, so that it cannot remember, even to reject, the themes of the tradition, Greek or Hebrew or Christian, by which our spiritual and aesthetic life has been nourished for two millennia or so. Tone poems about hydroelectric power stations or existentialist outcries against absurdity that are so private as to be solipsistic and self-indulgent are no substitute for the living tradition, nor are they a "poetry and philosophy of insight."

It is likewise from tradition that artistic creativity learns to know the liberation that can come only through discipline and a recognition of boundaries. The relation of Richard Wagner to tradition was, to put it mildly, a profoundly ambivalent one. In most of the canon of his work, he felt qualified to recast medieval traditions—classical, Germanic, Jewish, Christian, and various mixtures of these—in conformity with his own murky religiosity. He also believed, as did Nietzsche when he wrote *The Birth of Tragedy from the Spirit of Music*, that in the new medium of the "music drama" he was creating a form that would replace the traditions of both music and drama in the opera with something new. But, in spite of himself, it was not in any of his epic works, but in *Die Meistersinger von Nürnberg*, that he displayed the most penetrating and creative insight into tradition and into its distinction both from a pedantic traditionalism and from an arbitrary subjectivity.

Beckmesser, who is Wagner's caricature of his critics, professes to uphold the tradition but succeeds only in making himself ridiculous; Walther, who is the embodiment of raw talent, without form and void, wants to elevate his creativity and insight over the tradition of the masters, but manages almost to lose both the contest and Eva. But Hans Sachs, who is speaking for Wagner himself, cures Walther of his contempt for traditional rules by gently guiding him into a creativity that is fulfilled through, and not in spite of, the limits of a living tradition. As Sachs says in his closing soliloquy, "Do not, I say, despise the masters, but honor their art" and tradition! Having earlier cited the hostility of the traditionalists to Stravinsky's *Rite of Spring*, I must go on to point out what Stravinsky himself never tired of pointing out: that he could not have defied the tradition as he did unless he had first learned discipline from the tradition—which was why he urged that "Bach's cantatas . . . should be the centre of our repertoire"—so that he saw himself, and others now have begun to see him, as its legitimate heir and faithful disciple.

For the dichotomy between tradition and insight breaks down under the weight of history itself. A "leap of progress" is not a standing broad jump, which begins at the line of where we are now; it is a running broad jump through where we have been to where we go next. The growth of insight—in science, in the arts, in philosophy and theology—has not come through progressively sloughing off more and more of tradition, as though insight would be purest and deepest when it has finally freed itself of the dead past. It simply has not worked that way in the history of the tradition, and it does not work that way now. By including the dead in the circle of discourse, we enrich the quality of the conversation. Of course we do not listen only to the dead, nor are we a tape recording of the tradition. That really would be the dead faith of the living, not the living faith of the dead. But we do acquire the "insight" for which Emerson was pleading when we learn to interact creatively with the "tradition" which he was denouncing. An older contemporary of Emerson's, whom Emerson rightly regarded as the wisest and most universal mind of the century (except, Emerson felt obliged to add, for "that velvet life he lived!"), Johann Wolfgang von Goethe, saw it all more deeply and said it all more clearly:

> What you have as heritage,
> Take now as task;
> For thus you will make it your own!

Notes

3:13   Richard Altman with Mervyn Kaufman, *The Making of a*
        Musical: "Fiddler on the Roof" (New York: Crown Publishers,
        1971), p. 31. (Italics are my own.)

4:20   On the eleventh edition of *Britannica*, see Herman Kogan,
        The Great EB: The Story of the Encyclopædia Britannica (Chicago:
        University of Chicago Press, 1958), pp. 167–80.

5:29   Josef Pieper, *Über den Begriff der Tradition* (Cologne: West-
        deutscher Verlag, 1958), pp. 13–20; especially interesting to
        an American reader is Pieper's discussion, p. 15, of the
        English usage: "to hand down" a tradition.

5:31   The most comprehensive, and for my purposes the most
        helpful, of the modern works on the subject is Yves M.-J.
        Congar, *Tradition and Traditions: An Historical and a Theologi-*
        cal Essay, translated by Michael Naseby and Thomas Rain-
        borough (New York: Macmillan Company, 1967), with ex-
        tensive bibliographies.

6:7   The meaning of tradition for the social sciences (but also for
        the humanities) has been set forth with learning and insight

84   *Notes*

in Edward Shils, *Tradition* (Chicago: University of Chicago Press, 1981).

6:14 Claude Lévi-Strauss, *The Raw and the Cooked*, translated by John and Doreen Weightman (New York: Harper and Row, 1969).

6:29 S. N. Eisenstadt, "Post-Traditional Societies and the Continuity and Reconstruction of Tradition," *Daedalus* 102 (1973): 1–27; Jessie G. Lutz and Salah El-Shakhs, Introduction to *Tradition and Modernity: The Role of Traditionalism in the Modernization Process* (Washington, D.C.: University Press of America, 1982), pp. 1–5.

7:15 Milman Parry, *The Making of Homeric Verse*, edited by Adam Parry (Oxford: Clarendon Press, 1971).

8:4 Rebecca West, *Black Lamb and Grey Falcon: A Journey through Yugoslavia*, 2 vols. (New York: Viking, 1961), 2:1044.

8:6 Augustine *Confessions* 9.27.38.

8:10 Francis Cornford, *From Religion to Philosophy: A Study in the Origins of Western Speculation* (New York: Harper Torchbooks, 1957); Jane Ellen Harrison, *Themis: A Study of the Social Origins of Greek Religion* (Cambridge: Cambridge University Press, 1912), especially the "Excursus on the Ritual Forms Preserved in Greek Tragedy," pp. 341–63; Gilbert Murray, *Greek Studies* (Oxford: Clarendon Press, 1946), particularly the essays "Prolegomena to the Study of Ancient Philosophy" and "The 'Tradition,' or Handing Down, of Greek Literature."

8:15 For an account of the history of New Testament scholarship, see Werner Georg Kümmel, *The New Testament: The History of the Investigation of Its Problems*, translated by S. McLean Gilmour and Howard C. Kee (Nashville: Abingdon Press, 1972).

8:18 Augustine *Harmony of the Gospels* 1.3.5–6.

8:30 Augustine *Harmony of the Gospels* 1.4.7.

9:2   Rudolf Bultmann, *The History of the Synoptic Tradition*, 2d
        ed., translated by John Marsh (New York: Harper and Row,
        1968).

9:7   Hans Werner Bartsch, ed., *Kerygma and Myth*, 2d ed., trans-
        lated by Reginald H. Fuller (New York: Harper and Row,
        1961).

9:14   Pierre Grelot, "Tradition as Source and Environment of
        Scripture," in *The Dynamism of Biblical Tradition*, vol. 20 of
        Concilium (New York: Paulist Press, 1967).

9:22   Jaroslav Pelikan, *Luther the Expositor: Introduction to the Re-
        former's Exegetical Writings* (Saint Louis, Mo.: Concordia
        Publishing House, 1959), pp. 83–84. (Hereafter cited as
        Luther the Expositor.)

9:28   Heiko Augustinus Oberman, *Forerunners of the Reformation:
        The Shape of Late Medieval Thought Illustrated by Key Docu-
        ments* (1966; reprint, Philadelphia: Fortress Press, 1981).

10:13   The first critical edition of the works of William of Ockham,
        being published by the Franciscan Institute in Saint Bona-
        venture, New York, is nearing completion; the edition of
        Nicholas of Cusa, begun by the Heidelberg Academy of
        Sciences in 1932, has likewise been resumed.

10:22   See the essays collected in *The Reformation in Medieval Per-
        spective*, edited by Steven E. Ozment (Chicago: Quadrangle
        Books, 1971).

10:28   See, for example, Regin Prenter's discussion of "Luther
        and the Traditional Doctrine of the Trinity," in *Spiritus
        Creator*, translated by John M. Jensen (Philadelphia: For-
        tress Press, 1953), pp. 173–84.

11:7   *Luther the Expositor*, p. 33.

11:11   George Huntston Williams, "Joseph Priestley on Luther,"
        and Ernest B. Koenker, "Søren Kierkegaard on Luther," in
        Interpreters of Luther: Essays in Honor of Wilhelm Pauck, edited
        by Jaroslav Pelikan (Philadelphia: Fortress Press, 1968),
        pp. 121–58; 231–52.

11:18   Jaroslav Pelikan, *The Christian Tradition: A History of the Development of Doctrine*, 4 vols. to date (Chicago: University of Chicago Press, 1971–), 4:332–47. (Hereafter cited as *The Christian Tradition*.)

11:27   Perry Miller, *Errand into the Wilderness* (New York: Harper Torchbooks, 1964), p. 147.

12:3   Perry Miller, *Roger Williams: His Contribution to the American Tradition* (New York: Atheneum, 1962), p. 38.

12:18   Jaroslav Pelikan, "The Doctrine of the Image of God," in *The Common Christian Roots of the European Nations: An International Colloquium in the Vatican*, 2 vols. (Florence: Le Monnier, 1982), 1:53–62.

13:20   Nicholas [Nicolas] Berdyaev, *The Russian Idea* (New York: Macmillan Company, 1948).

13:27   Ljubomir Tadić, *Tradicija i revolucija* (Belgrade: Srpska književna Zadruga, 1972), especially "Reformation and Revolution," pp. 38–60; Siegfried Wollgast, "Tradition und Widerspruch, Tradition und Fortschritt," in *Tradition und Philosophie: Über die Tradition in Vergangenheit und Zukunft* (Berlin, 1975), pp. 48–58.

14:17   *The Christian Tradition*, 1:12–27.

14:20   Karl Holl, "Die schriftstellerische Form des griechischen Heiligenlebens," in *Gesammelte Aufsätze zur Kirchengeschichte*, 3 vols. (1928; reprint, Darmstadt: Wissenschaftliche Buchgesellschaft, 1964), 2:249–69.

15:4   Jacob Burckhardt, *The Civilization of the Renaissance in Italy*, 2 vols. (New York: Harper Torchbooks, 1958), 1:175–278.

15:11   Heinrich Fichtenau, *The Carolingian Empire: The Age of Charlemagne*, translated by Peter Munz (New York: Harper Torchbooks, 1964), pp. 98–103.

15:12   Charles Homer Haskins, *The Renaissance of the Twelfth Century* (New York: New American Library, 1976), pp. 93–126.

15:28   *The Christian Tradition*, 1:5.

16:9   William A. Wallace, *Prelude to Galileo: Essays on Medieval and Sixteenth-Century Sources of Galileo's Thought* (Boston: D. Reidel, 1981).

16:30   Cf. Jaroslav Pelikan, *Historical Theology: Continuity and Change in Christian Doctrine* (New York: Corpus Instrumentorum, 1971), p. 88. (Hereafter cited as *Historical Theology*.)

17:15   See *The Christian Tradition*, 1:339.

17:17   Gilbert Keith Chesterton, *Orthodoxy* (Garden City, N.Y.: Image Books, 1959), p. 48.

18:6   See the passages cited in *Historical Theology*, p. 16.

.19:1   *The Christian Tradition*, 4:19–21.

19:5   *The Christian Tradition*, 4:224.

19:19   Immanuel Kant, *The Metaphysic of Morals*, chap. 11.

19:30   Czeslaw Milosz, *Nobel Lecture* (New York: Farrar, Straus and Giroux, 1980), p. 14.

20:21   Edmund Burke, *Reflections on the Revolution in France*, edited by Conor Cruise O'Brien (New York: Penguin English Library, 1982), pp. 194–95.

24:13   Czeslaw Milosz, *Nobel Lecture*, p. 14.

24:23   Among the many works on the subject, cf. Günter Biemer, *Newman on Tradition*, translated by Kevin Smyth (New York: Herder and Herder, 1967), especially pp. 33–67 on the development of Newman's view of tradition.

25:1   John Henry Newman, *Apologia Pro Vita Sua: Being a History of His Religious Opinions*, edited by Martin J. Svaglic (Oxford: Clarendon Press, 1967), p. 178.

25:5   I have used the first edition, published in London in 1833; hereafter I shall cite this edition as *Arians* with page number, retaining Newman's own spelling, capitalization, and use of italics (unless otherwise indicated).

25:18   Louis Bouyer, *Newman: His Life and Spirituality*, translated by J. Lewis May (New York: Meridian Books, 1960), p. 162.

25:21   Jaroslav Pelikan, *Development of Christian Doctrine: Some His-*

torical *Prolegomena* (New Haven: Yale University Press, 1969); *Scholarship and Its Survival* (Princeton: Carnegie Foundation for the Advancement of Teaching, 1983).

26:7   John Henry Newman, *The Arians of the Fourth Century*, 3d ed. (London: E. Lumley, 1871), pp. 260–61, n. 5.

26:11   For a history of the Council of Nicea and the trinitarian theology of Athanasius, cf. "The Mystery of the Trinity," in *The Christian Tradition*, 1:172–225.

26:12   Newman, *Arians*, p. 147.

26:15   John Henry Newman, *An Essay on the Development of Christian Doctrine*, edited by Charles Frederick Harrold (New York: Longmans, Green and Company, 1949), p. 134.

26:21   Newman, *Arians*, p. 151.

27:2   Newman, *Arians*, p. 148.

27:4   Newman, *Arians*, p. 60.

27:10   Newman, *Arians*, pp. 148–49.

27:16   Newman, *Arians*, p. 237.

27:22   Newman, *Arians*, p. 160.

27:27   Newman, *Arians*, p. 40.

27:28   Newman, *Arians*, p. 147.

27:31   Newman, *Arians*, p. 39.

28:5   Newman, *Arians*, p. 41.

28:9   Newman, *Arians*, p. 252.

28:12   Newman, *Arians*, p. 196.

28:13   Newman, *Arians*, p. 165.

28:17   Newman, *Arians*, p. 163.

28:20   Newman, *Arians*, p. 391.

28:23   Newman, *Arians*, p. 41.

28:31   Newman, *Arians*, pp. 139–40.

29:8   Newman, *Arians*, p. 75.

29:12   Newman, *Arians*, p. 247.

29:18   Newman, *Arians*, p. 204.

29:21   Newman, *Arians*, p. 175.

29:24   Newman, *Arians*, p. 76.

29:27   Newman, *Arians*, p. 39.

30:1   Newman, *Arians*, p. 196.

30:3   Newman, *Arians*, p. 298.

30:8   Newman, *Arians*, p. 378.

30:13   Newman, *Arians*, p. 158.

30:15   Newman, *Arians*, p. 381.

30:25   Newman, *Arians*, p. 62.

30:28   Newman, *Arians*, p. 192.

30:31   Newman, *Arians*, p. 359.

31:3   Newman, *Arians*, p. 223.

31:6   Newman, *Arians*, pp. 68–69.

31:11   Isaiah 9:6.

31:22   Newman, *Arians*, pp. 55–56.

31:27   Newman, *Arians*, p. 61.

31:29   Newman, *Arians*, p. 240.

32:7   Newman, *Arians*, p. 34.

32:17   Newman, *Arians*, p. 164.

32:28   Newman, *Arians*, pp. 237–38.

33:1   Owen Chadwick, *From Bossuet to Newman: The Idea of Doctrinal Development* (Cambridge: Cambridge University Press, 1957), p. 235.

33:6   Newman, *Arians*, p. 209 (italics added).

33:10   Newman, *Arians*, p. 366.

33:15   Newman, *Arians*, p. 244 (italics added).

33:31   Newman, *Arians*, p. 88.

34:3   John Henry Newman, *An Essay in Aid of a Grammar of Assent* (Garden City, N.Y.: Image Books, 1955), p. 329.

34:15   Newman, *Arians*, p. 166.

34:21   Newman, *Arians*, p. 96.

34:26   Newman, *Arians*, p. 88.

34:30   Newman, *Arians*, pp. 100–01.

35:10   Newman, *Arians*, pp. 89–91.

35:26   Newman, *Arians*, p. 51.

36:6   Newman, *Arians*, p. 60.

36:10   Newman, *Arians*, p. 285.

36:14   Newman, *Arians*, p. 1.

36:18   Newman, *Arians*, p. 9.

36:20   Newman, *Arians*, p. 144.

36:22   Newman, *Arians*, p. 190.

36:29   Newman, *Arians*, p. 140.

37:3   Newman, *Arians*, pp. 306–07.

37:6   Newman, *Arians*, pp. 12, 421.

37:10   Newman, *Arians*, 3d ed. (London, 1871), p. vi; the appendix is on p. 478.

37:23   Cf. Newman, *Essay on Development* (Harrold ed.), p. 421.

38:4   Newman, *Arians*, p. 285.

38:9   Newman, *Arians*, p. 390.

38:13   Newman, *Arians*, p. 27.

38:28   Newman, *Arians*, p. 195.

39:6   Etienne Gilson, Introduction to Newman, *Grammar of Assent* (Image ed.), p. 18.

39:18   Congar, *Tradition and Traditions*, p. 211.

39:26   Newman, *Arians*, p. 146.

40:6   Newman, *Essay on Development* (Harrold ed.), p. 7.

43:14   Daniel J. Boorstin, *The Lost World of Thomas Jefferson* (Boston: Beacon Press, 1960), pp. 225–26.

44:4   Cf. *Luther the Expositor*, pp. 71–88.

44:18   John M. Headley, *Luther's View of Church History* (New Haven: Yale University Press, 1963), p. 51.

44:22   Paul Oskar Kristeller, *Renaissance Thought: The Classic, Scholastic, and Humanistic Strains* (New York: Harper Torchbooks, 1961), p. 79.

45:5   Claude Welch, *In This Name: The Doctrine of the Trinity in Contemporary Theology* (New York: Charles Scribner's Sons, 1952), pp. 3–9.

45:24   Isaiah Berlin, Foreword to Friedrich Meinecke, *Historism:*

The Rise of a New Historical Outlook, translated by J. E. Anderson (New York: Herder and Herder, 1972), p. ix.

45:31   René Wellek, *A History of Modern Criticism: 1750–1950,* 4 vols. to date (New Haven: Yale University Press, 1955–), 1:27–30.

46:12   Karl Löwith, *Von Hegel zu Nietzsche* (Zurich: Europa Verlag, 1941), pp. 44–48.

46:23   Karl Barth, *Protestant Thought: From Rousseau to Ritschl,* translated by H. H. Hartwell with an introduction by Jaroslav Pelikan (New York: Harper and Row, 1959), p. 311 (translation slightly revised).

47:10   Lucio da Veiga Coutinho, *Tradition et histoire dans la controverse moderniste, 1898–1910* (Rome: Gregorian University, 1954).

47:12   Lefferts A. Loetscher, *The Broadening Church: A Study of Theological Issues in the Presbyterian Church since 1869* (Philadelphia: University of Pennsylvania Press, 1957), pp. 48–74.

47:29   See Meinecke's masterful analysis of Goethe, *Historism,* pp. 373–495.

48:10   *Environmental Factors in Christian History,* edited by John Thomas McNeill et al. (Chicago: University of Chicago Press, 1939).

49:25   Edward Gibbon, *The History of the Decline and Fall of the Roman Empire,* 7 vols., edited by J. B. Bury (London: Methuen and Company, 1896–1900), 5:132.

50:10   Adolf von Harnack, "In memoriam: Karl Holl," in *Aus der Werkstatt des Vollendeten* (Giessen: Alfred Töpelmann, 1930), p. 285.

51:20   Deuteronomy 6:4.

52:31   See the posthumously published work by Ernst Troeltsch, *Der Historismus und seine Überwindung: Fünf Vorträge* (Berlin: Pan Verlag, Rolf Heise, 1924).

54:17   Galatians 4:26.

54:22   Charles Norris Cochrane, *Christianity and Classical Culture: A Study of Thought and Expression from Augustus to Augustine* (London: Oxford University Press, 1944), pp. 213–60.

54:30   See *The Christian Tradition*, 2:91–145.

56:20   Clifford Geertz, *The Interpretation of Cultures: Selected Essays* (New York: Basic Books, 1973), p. 219.

57:26   Exodus 32:19.

57:28   Plato *Apology* 38.

57:30   Matthew 19:17.

59:5   *Enchiridion symbolorum definitionum et declarationum de rebus fidei et morum*, 32d ed., edited by Heinrich Denzinger and Adolf Schönmetzer (Freiburg im Breisgau: Herder, 1963), p. 601.

60:22   Pascal *Pensées* 6.397.

61:10   Chesterton, *Orthodoxy*, p. 79.

61:13   Chesterton, *Orthodoxy*, pp. 47–48.

65:4   *The Christian Tradition*, 1:9.

65:10   Ralph Waldo Emerson, *Nature*, in *The Complete Essays and Other Writings of Ralph Waldo Emerson*, edited by Brooks Atkinson (New York: Modern Library, 1940), p. 3.

66:2   Ralph Waldo Emerson, "An Address," in *Complete Essays*, p. 81.

66:11   Ralph Waldo Emerson, "Phi Beta Kappa Address," in *Complete Essays*, pp. 45–63.

66:27   Burckhardt, *Civilization of the Renaissance*, 1:257.

66:30   Andrew Dickson White, *A History of the Warfare of Science with Theology in Christendom*, 2 vols. (New York: D. Appleton and Company, 1896); the work has been reprinted often.

68:11   Etienne Ménard, *La Tradition: Révélation, Ecriture, Eglise selon Saint Thomas d'Aquin* (Paris: Desclée de Brouwer, 1964), especially the word study of *tradere* and cognates in Thomas, pp. 13–46.

69:8   Cf. *The Christian Tradition*, 3:216–29.

69:19   Romola Nijinsky, *Nijinsky* (New York: Simon and Schuster, 1934), pp. 201–05.
70:11   Igor Stravinsky and Robert Craft, *Expositions and Develop-ments* (Berkeley and Los Angeles: University of California Press, 1981), pp. 142–43.
71:8   2 Corinthians 3:6.
71:26   Augustine *City of God* 11.9.
71:28   Thomas Aquinas *Summa Theologica* 1.74.2.
72:9   See *Historical Theology*, pp. 136–37, on this translation and exegesis of Romans 5:12.
73:16   Cf. *The Christian Tradition*, 2:75–90.
74:2   Georges V. Florovsky, "The Function of Tradition in the Ancient Church," in *Bible, Church, Tradition: An Eastern Orthodox View* (Belmont, Mass.: Nordland, 1972), pp. 73–92; cf. Yves-Noël Lelouvier, *Perspectives russes sur l'église* (Paris: Editions du Centurion, 1968), pp. 107–20.
75:19   *The Christian Tradition*, 2:70–75.
76:5   Alfred North Whitehead, *Science and the Modern World* (New York: New American Library, 1948), pp. 49–50.
78:12   Etienne Gilson, "Pourquoi saint Thomas a critiqué saint Augustin," *Archives d'histoire doctrinale et littéraire du Moyen Age*, 1 (1926): 5–127.
78:27   Eugene D. Genovese, *Roll, Jordan, Roll: The World the Slaves Made* (New York: Pantheon Books, 1974).
79:1   Thomas Kuhn, *The Structure of Scientific Revolutions*, 2d ed. (Chicago: University of Chicago Press, 1970).
79:4   *Johann Kepler, 1571–1620: A Tercentenary Commemoration of His Life and Work* (Baltimore: History of Science Society, 1931), especially the essay by E. H. Johnson, "Kepler and Mysticism"; Frank Edward Manuel, *The Religion of Isaac Newton* (Oxford: Clarendon Press, 1974).
81:15   Igor Stravinsky and Robert Craft, *Conversations with Igor Stravinsky* (Berkeley and Los Angeles: University of California Press, 1980), p. 31.
82:11   Goethe *Faust* 682–83. (The free translation is my own.)